Chanel Solitaire

CHANEL
Solitaire

by CLAUDE BAILLÉN
translated from the French
by Barbara Bray

Quadrangle/The New York Times Book Co.
10 East 53 Street, New York, N. Y. 10022

The photographs on pp. 8, 11, 12, 13, 14, 111, 142, 154 and
171 are by Jacques Robert; those on pp. 31 and 32 are from
the Collection R. Tubiana; that on p. 129 by Mike de Dulmen,
Paris; all photographs are from the private collection of
Madame Gabrielle Labrunie, Mademoiselle Chanel's great-niece.

First published in France under the title *Chanel Solitaire*
First published in the United States 1974
© 1971 by Editions Gallimard
© in the English translation by Wm Collins Sons & Co Ltd 1973

ISBN 0-8129-0474-5
Library of Congress Catalog Card Number 74-78651

Set in Monotype Garamond

For information, address Quadrangle/The New York Times
Book Co. 10 East 53 Street, New York, New York 10022

Manufactured in the United States of America

Contents

Foreword

This book derives from my friendship with
Coco Chanel during the last ten years of her life.
It is entirely subjective and based on experience.

I met her in the rue Cambon towards the close
of her life. She was so intense, so riveting in her
despotic little boater, emerging from her mirrored
stairway, that I dimly caught her essential aroma,
and the even more illicit scent of an eternal youth.

I parted from her at the door of the Ritz on the
eve of her death.

The Fugitive

Sever all shackles and set off with
outstretched hands.
PIERRE REVERDY, *Le Voleur de talan*

'Two lifesize Renaissance Venetian blackamoors ceremoniously pointed the way'

The Fugitive

As soon as the door opened two lifesize Renaissance Venetian blackamoors ceremoniously pointed the way from plinths of beaten gold, their palms emerging from rich cuffs piped with blue. She ran her fingers dreamily over their lapels. 'They're live people, you know – they're my companions.' Mirrors everywhere. Crystal chandeliers lit up the Chinese screens in the ante-room. At the threshold of the salon more screens rose up beside the huge sofa of fawn suède where she took refuge. I never saw her sit anywhere else. Opposite were two eighteenth-century French gilt armchairs with neutral suède upholstery: low-legged – Chanel loathed all that was stilted, pretentious, conventional. Before her stood a low lacquer table covered with chased enamel boxes bearing the Westminster family arms. 'Look – the outside's enamel and what's most precious, the gold, is inside.' Scattered over the table were her various pairs of glasses; the gold manes of her zodiacal lions glittered. Her self-made paradise unveiled itself, a marvellous and incomparable miscellany. 'The main thing is, the elements themselves should be beautiful.' Cats from China, eyes ringed with mystery, crouched against sombre lacquer, between crystal frog and purple tiger; there were winged ducks, looming camels; Kruschev, her little Fabergé pig made of coral, rested his insolent snout on the evening papers. The last editions awaited her, folded, on the black fur rug. She settled among the cushions and fell on *France-Soir*, plunging into the dew of the news. 'I need the plebs.' Ancient lives from Plutarch to Shakespeare looked down on her; all her own lifetime stretched out in bindings of black and beige. Her seasons numbered no winter of the mind. Dali's gold ear of corn embellished the dark wall. An Egyptian mask ravished the silence.

Lipchitz's fire-dogs challenged the magic Afghans on her desk. Other guards of iron enclosed the leaping fire. Naked caryatids – ships' figureheads – rose to the ceiling holding sheaves of wheat or a chubby infant. A pale Greek marble Venus, bosom bent forward, stood out against the mirror over the fireplace. A black meteorite embodied fear, a gilt wooden monkey its own existence, a lion challenge. Vast folds of Chinese screens advanced, unfurling forests, characters erudite and indecipherable, a bronze doe and buck the colour of late autumn. The solitary arranged her pets in couples. 'I've loved Chinese screens ever since I was eighteen. I thought I'd faint with joy the first time I saw a Coromandel in a showroom.'

'How did you get to like Chinese art, Mademoiselle?'

'I don't know. There's something compelling and irrevocable about it that appealed to me. Screens were the first thing I ever bought. You don't come across them much in the provinces, of course. I'd never seen anything like it. The people I knew were more likely to buy a store-cupboard for sheets dried in the sun.'

On the red lacquer table two antique does with astonished eyes, a saddled horse and its mate, flanked a long strip of ancient cloth of gold weighed down with amber pilgrims, dim as dream. Allah's paradise. An Indian buddha, slim and severe, held a lotus in his folded hands. An African statuette of a Fenosa flute-girl piped its tune beside a lump of rock-crystal.

The brown jute curtains were drawn. Outside, the flag flew over the municipal buildings and infant school of the rue Cambon. 'Wild horses wouldn't get me to dine out.' The lamp-lit table always expected a friend. Dinner was thought up at the last minute – sippets and soft-scrambled eggs, chicken New Orléans. It would go round somehow. 'A home that isn't ready for anything is a prison.' Secretly Bohemian, she scorned all rules. 'I hate habit. One should never live by

Opposite, 'Crystal chandeliers lit up Chinese screens'

'Beside the huge sofa of fawn suede . . . stood a low
lacquer table covered with chased enamel boxes bearing
the Westminster family arms'

habit.' She addressed herself seriously to the white meat and
two spoonfuls of sweet corn. 'I can't bear bad cooking . . .
if the salmon trout isn't all that it might be . . . How awful . . .'
Was it from the province of her birth that she got her keen
and infallible sense of food?

'I need to feed,' she said, on the way to the dining-room.
City imposture was banned. Her table served potatoes baked
in embers and crackling in their silver foil; purée made of
fresh chestnuts; as winter desserts, dates and figs mashed in
cream. One day there was baked grapefruit, but she pulled a
face. 'I dislike grapefruit and things grown in cotton-wool.
Fruit should be eaten in season – ripe apricots and nectarines.'
Asparagus in November infuriated her. 'You know I loathe
forced vegetables. Tasteless. And the price!' Onions were
taboo: 'I don't like food that repeats on you.' Colette once
tried to persuade her to eat an onion. 'No, thanks!' 'Go on,
you only have to eat a couple of coffee-beans or a few grapes
afterwards.' No use. Chanel didn't trifle with the senses; she

'A pale Greek marble Venus . . . stood out against the mirror over the fireplace'

defended them ruthlessly. 'The cook will soon see what I'm made of. Trying to be fancy! What does she take this for, a wedding breakfast?' One day she wouldn't touch lunch: tournedos with French beans – 'This is what's known as good plain cooking, for a houseful of children. The very thing I detest.' The offender's fate was sealed. 'I don't propose to fight with meat. I fight with my thoughts. It's terrible. Soon they'll be bringing me in a portion on a plate, like a navvy. Ten years ago I lived in luxury. One minute elegance, the next a railway buffet.'

Intermediaries did the lopping off of heads: she only decreed the executions, she didn't burden herself with carrying them out. Monsieur Tranchant got a new cook, fired the maid, did the paying out. 'I call him the headsman.' But axing others didn't save him from being chewed up himself. 'Old boar,' she'd rage, or, feeling less sylvan, 'Commercial traveller!'

She reached out for caraway seeds, currant bread, rusks. No cannibalism, and no 'family cooking.' No ceremony to kill

Mirror from a Spanish sacristy above console table representing one of the
Seasons

confidence. 'What a to-do just now with Serge Lifar! If I'd so much as sighed while he was working he'd have screamed. If he thinks I like working under those lights . . .' A drop of Russian vodka tinted her skin with gaiety. A couple of fingers was enough. She liked vodka because it was made from wheat, but didn't drink spirits. 'I often tell myself – you're no Russian, my girl!' Her table was served by honest, unpretentious wines: chilled Riesling, cool Chianti or Beaujolais, a good Bordeaux for guests. She hated warm wine. Gold shells held cigarettes in their fluting; her couched lions lay on the bare fleshy wood of the table; the silverware shone, the initials CC plain and simple; the white plates were edged with two black C's interlaced. 'No regimentation! It doesn't improve either the knife or the food. It's simple things that are beautiful. Everything else is sophistication, sham.' Beside her place there was always a little Chinese monkey of white porcelain.

Mirrors from a Spanish sacristy flashed their dazzling crystal drops. She brought them back from Italy and later discovered they'd once been part of the treasures of the church in Seville, precious stones suspended between heaven and earth. Console tables supported by nymphs of gilded wood rose up from pedestals of clay. They were the Seasons. She'd been able to get only two of them, in Venice at the Casati auction. Was it chance? Chanel dressed only the youth of the riper seasons, spring and autumn, as though cold and heat, bareness and sheaf, were linked by an instinctive inter-action. On the floor, a black Savonnerie carpet covered with crimson roses. The doors were hung with jute: 'They were ugly. I did away with them.'

Receptive and profound, she proffered her face. Over the feline fold of the nostrils the eyes were deep and watchful. She fascinated herself, saw things, ransacked them. Cocteau said: she looks at you fondly, then slaughters you. He knew, she said, that it was his poetry I sentenced to death. Her passion knew nothing of tact. Only people she knew were welcome. Ornament was not for her. All that interested her was the pistol shot of truth.

Conversation was a bright fire, catching quickly and burning right down to the evening embers. Her full-blooded rebelliousness revealed refusal and rejection deep beneath her wit, as if she were still in the throes of the struggle. Yet always she'd escaped. Any danger was better than the danger of staying put. 'You can't live within limited bounds,' she said to me one day. 'It stifles you. You must charge through.'

As she did, in her youth. As a girl she spent some holidays at Vichy, where her grandfather took the waters. The Baroness de Nexon, her favourite aunt and her grandparents' nineteenth child, was not yet married. She had a wasp waist and bows in her hair, and took Coco to a tea-party where her one fear was being seized by the giggles. There Coco met Etienne Balsan, one of the most influential men of the day. They talked about horses – horses and bad luck. Her bad luck was that she and her sister were being brought up by their maternal aunts. Their widowed father had gone to America. 'I'm going to kill myself,' she told Balsan. 'All through my childhood I wanted to be loved. Every day I thought about how to kill myself. The viaduct, perhaps . . . They'd be sorry for a little while. But *I*'d be dead!' What she was eager for now was not death but escape. Balsan invited her to see his stables at Saint-Ouen and the abbey at Royal Lieu. Even more than by what she said, he was moved by her smooth skin, her untamed yet gentle air, the warm curls under the pulled-down hat, the bold nostrils and the way she suddenly dropped her eye-lids when her expression deepened. 'There's nothing to be frightened of,' he said. 'I only like old ladies.' 'I'll come with you,' she said. 'Just give me time to pack my case.'

Her whole fortune consisted of an alpaca suit for summer, a Cheviot one for winter, and a goatskin jacket. But her suitcase was full of illusions from all the novels she'd read. 'You don't know the damage country attics can do to the imagina-

Adrienne de Nexon, Coco's favourite aunt

tion.' It was there her aunts had stowed away all the news-
papers and tied together with string copies of *Illustration*.
Coco devoured novels in instalments and serial stories. 'I had
one teacher,' she told me. 'A sentimental ninny. Pierre
Decourcelle.' Her heroines in the novels became her counter-
parts. The girl was thrilled by the lady in white who, feeling
warm at the races, takes off her long jacket to reveal an
exquisite blouse, or dresses all in astrakhan with a toque of
parma violets. She would never wear them herself. But her
pulsing heart had taught her the wicked are the good, and
to hate the bourgeoisie. Already she made her escape from the
gloomy regimented universe ruled by her crabbed aunts, defending, in the small corner of her solitude, an existence
fortified and impregnable. To listen to her was almost like
listening to that other country girl, Colette. 'That was me in
my youth: the run of a library where all was grist, but you
couldn't have found any "suitable" reading for me whether
at six or at ten or at fourteen. Forbidden books, books too
serious, books too light. Rather boring books, and dazzling
ones that suddenly lit up and drew the enchanted child within
·their portals. The randomness itself was noble. Each book,
though imperfectly assimilated at the time, was a conquest.
One day its jungle of words and ideas would open on to a
calm and friendly landscape.'

Coco caught a glimpse of it and set off boldly for Balsan's
château. His old mistress, Emilienne d'Alençon, lived there in
heavy gowns and spotted veils. She wasn't much disturbed
by the new arrival, who thought of nothing but riding and
whose only mirror was the horizon. Balsan burst out laughing
when Coco told him she rode bareback. She wore stable-
boy's breeches, caught the horse by the mane, and dismounted
by sliding down over its tail. 'You were brought up in a circus,'
cried Balsan. But she outdid the real stable-boys, who were
afraid to mount the animal. 'What about a gallop on the
two-year-old?' he asked. So off she raced through the forest
of Compiègne, the sandy fragrant forest where she rode every

day. 'If someone brought me a branch from the forest of Compiègne I'd recognise the smell straight away. I didn't know any people; I knew the horses. I thought it so pretty, the way they threw out their legs in front of them.' Her hands made the gesture of untwining and flying forward. At Royal Lieu she dressed 'neither as great lady nor as scullery-maid': she wore trousers, and discovered the meaning of clothes. The young girl heard the racecourse gossip, read all the gazettes, and ordered little hacking jackets from the tailor in La Croix Saint-Ouen. 'Emilienne d'Alençon used to ask me, "Well, are you happy?" I answered, "I'm neither happy nor unhappy – I'm hiding. It's like home here, only better."' She was in mortal terror of the local police. Had she only half escaped from her aunts? They thought she was at her grandparents', who, until they found out, thought she was back in the strict old fold. Coco wrote to her young aunt Adrienne de Nexon for the money for her train fare. What was her horror when the answer came: 'Whatever you do keep out of the way or they'll put you in a reformatory.' This other life had come too close upon her childhood. 'If it hadn't been for the riding I'd have left. But I hadn't enough money. If I'd had just a bit more I'd have gone back.' In the evening she used to fall asleep at the table and weep – at her aunts' she'd have been in bed two hours by that time. 'I'll take you home,' said Balsan. 'I'll tell them I'm bringing you back just as I found you and you're still only a little girl.' His answer was in the tears of humiliation in her eyes.

The fabulous rider's supple future was already approaching. She'd learned to ride side-saddle, and they went hunting in Pau. Coco met Boy Capel, and fell under the spell of the marvellous Englishman with green eyes and black hair. 'All happened in looks' in the stripped garden of her eyes, which could also reflect the jealousy of an animal betrayed. Impelled by a loveless childhood and the irresistible instinct to give all, she entered into the dominion of men.

'Are you leaving to-morrow?'

'Yes.'

'I'm coming with you.'

'My dear child, I'll have to speak to Etienne.'

'He knows. I've written.'

In the note she held out, Boy Capel read: 'My dear Etienne, I shall never be able to repay the kindness and comfort you've given me while I've been with you . . .' She tried in vain to explain she wasn't his mistress: Boy wouldn't listen. Coco was at the station with her suitcase and hopped on the train. Three days later Balsan arrived in Paris. He'd discovered he loved her.

The two men quarrelled over and forgot her, but she had only one idea: to become independent. There was no question of letting herself be put on a rein. She was looked after by Mademoiselle de Saint-Pons, secretary of the doctor in whose charge Boy had put her. 'Anything so long as she enjoys herself,' Boy told the secretary, 'but don't let her change.' Balsan delicately went off to spend a year in the Argentine. Capel's mistresses asked when he was going to leave her. 'I'd rather cut my leg off,' he answered.

The girl's naturalness was disarming. At the Ritz, where they'd taken refuge, she saw a lift for the first time in her life and didn't know if one was supposed to greet the people in it – whether it was for her or for them to speak. Her companion caught her distress signal and said with a wave of the hand, 'I'll explain.' 'He never did,' she said wistfully, with the eyes of a country girl still.

'Come now, woman,' Boy said to her. 'I can't pay the slightest addresses without people saying "But of course you're going to marry her." You a woman!' Their friend the doctor sensed the trouble between the young couple and soothed the girl's modesty. 'My dear child, I see women every day of the week. It's my job. I'm ready whenever you are.' A snip of the scissors cleared the threshold of her life as a woman. 'The seat of pleasure's a question of structure,' she told me. 'As far

'The girl's naturalness was disarming'

as I'm concerned, if it hadn't been for that little snip of the scissors . . . After that it didn't hurt any more.'

She ordered a dress from Cheruit in white and blue – 'I looked like the Virgin Mary' – which was horribly tight. She wore it to dine at the Café de Paris. After dinner, the grosgrain got so tight she asked her escort to undo her straitjacket at the waist. Then, impossible to do it up again or even to fill the breach. She hadn't an evening cloak, only a raincoat. She swore never to fall into that trap again, and she kept her word. The knell of grosgrain had sounded.

The horsewoman was going to show women the way of

freedom, replacing their paraphernalia with her own instinct for unconstraint. 'Nothing makes a woman look older than obvious expensiveness, ornateness, complication. I still dress as I always did, like a schoolgirl.' In the first decades of the century she created a sensation at the races, on the arm of her elegant companion, dressed in a navy blue suit like a girl from boarding-school in her Sunday best, with a boater perched on her rich black hair, amongst all the befeathered ladies. The slim little stranger, muscular from riding and free and easy in her short skirts, scorned corsets. 'When I wore those men's jackets and the boater, I had an Englishman for a lover: I didn't look at anyone, and the English threw themselves on me like poverty on the world. You see what good luck can do. I found myself in what's called society: polo, tennis, the races. I thought everyone was looking at the polo-players . . . But they were looking at me. When they saw that little monkey come on the scene . . . The women still used to tuck their skirts up!' She was just as mischievous over headgear. 'Hats? I bought them in the Galeries Lafayette and wore them perfectly straight – in those days they were usually tilted and covered with birds' nests. Everyone admired them, so I thought: why not actually make them?' She laughed, the boater of to-day firmly in place. She opened a hat shop in Deauville and was besieged. Women used to wear feather sun-bonnets to go on the beach. The times her aunts had lamented she had legs like a boy's! 'I dreamed of having legs like bottles . . . The calves of those women from the Auvergne! And their busts . . .' Her own slim breasts couldn't compare with the generous proportions of the cocottes. 'I liked the cocottes because they were pretty and scented and painted – I didn't like society women. I did my best to fill out the requisite space with what I had in front. The others' monumental bosoms overflowed. But no, it wasn't me at all!' Her body's refusal led her to invent her own natural style. 'I jump straight into my clothes, so what's needed are clothes that are good and becoming,' she decided. Her little jockey coats were in huge demand. 'We ought to have been on our guard against that boyish head. It was going to give us every kind of shock, and produce, out of its little conjuror's hat, gowns and coiffures and sweaters and jewels and boutiques,' sighed Poiret, the famous but soon discomfited couturier. Before these women ponderous and impressive as battleships, she was to appear in a scrap of humble, unknown jersey – in a sweater at Deauville, white trousers in Venice, a black dress at Ciro's. She opened in the rue Cambon, where she installed her magic Coromandels: the lacquer worked with the animal mysteries in gold was to be her setting above all others. An affinity had come into being, intimate and secret as a spring beneath the leaves.

Discovering fashion was an experience. A novelty that particularly thrilled her was having a cheque-book. She was amazed at her budding power. 'Everyone round me was so tactful, I thought I was making money – I thought I was rich.' Boy was desolate: she wouldn't talk about anything else but her shop. All the Russian émigrés descended upon her, and she was still wearing the same dress. 'What about spending something on yourself?' 'These people are very badly off,' she answered, 'and you know that costs a lot.' 'A bit too much,' said Boy. He was to repent those words.

They drove to Saint-Germain-en-Laye where Coco, after striding up and down the terrace, disappeared into the forest. 'We'll soon be at Maisons-Lafitte,' panted Boy, who hated walking. In vain he tried to reason with her. 'We'll be married, Coco – you know what's mine is yours.' She answered he could have dinner without her, she'd send the car back. No go. They drove back without exchanging a word in front of the 'mechanic', as she always called the driver, even later. 'I didn't say a word, but when we got back I threw my handbag and everything on the floor and said I was leaving. He caught me up outside Smith's – it was raining so hard I couldn't see where I was going – and then I started to cry. It was all over. I was going to the rue Cambon.' 'No, no,' he said. 'What for?

Come back and go to bed and calm down. You're like a ten-year-old.'

At three in the morning she woke saying 'I'm hungry.'

This dizzy leap from feeling to practical reality was to colour all her life. She herself clung to her mixture of aloofness and application, stunning luxury and ruthless attachment to the everyday.

Already her doctor, Professor Robin, sent her all his patients. One evening Boy took her to see Isabelle Mallet, who, like him, was a theosophist. Protestant high society invited her into their deferential homes, knowing he wouldn't come to dinner otherwise. 'Do you want the children to be there or not?' Blanche Hottinguer asked her. 'To be there, of course,' said Coco. 'Then be here at seven-thirty.' This austere, orderly atmosphere, with lots of children and well-set tables, reminded her of the provinces: 'I felt as if I was back home.' She sent for her dead sister's little boy, and Boy Capel called him his son. Every time he saw a barge on the Seine the child used to say to Coco, 'Look, that's ours.' Capel owned some boats which transported coal. 'Not ours, Boy's,' Coco would answer. 'But he told me you're going to marry him!'

Going to mass at six, cleaning the curé's boots, and helping the old servant had not been much of an education. Coco tried to play mother. When the boy made a rude noise after lunch she reprimanded him. 'Monsieur le Curé does it and says pardon,' answered the child, who loved the country priest better than anyone in the world. At night he cried his eyes out and wanted to go back to him. When Boy took him to lunch at the Rothschilds' he marched out of the nursery because the boys were wearing girls' shoes, and sat down at table with the grown-ups. When the finger-bowls were brought in, 'I've behaved very well up to now,' he said to Boy, 'but I'm not going to drink that!'

Boy decided to send him to his own school in England. He set out for Harrow, but went on to Beaumont, his Catholic guardian having kicked up an awful row about his being sent

Coco and her
nephew

to a Protestant school. 'The provinces!' sighed Coco. 'You don't know what it's like to get away from them!' She had taken to her heels and landed, accurate as a bird, far from the prim and proper malice, the invisible starvation that made Rimbaud revile the provinces as the place where people live off 'starch and mud.'

> *Around the square, trimmed into grudging lawns,*
> *Where all's correct, including trees and flowers,*
> *The wheezy bourgeois, choking with the heat,*
> *Air every Thursday night their envious follies.*

The governess-cart of her youth was left far behind. She bought a car, a dark blue Rolls upholstered in black leather. 'You don't think it's too funereal?' they asked in the show-rooms. It was the era of bad taste: people often had their cars upholstered in toile de Jouy, or watered silk, or lace! 'No. You'll see, everyone will be ordering cars like this.'

She spoke truer than she knew: she launched the fashion for dark cars. Her instinct carried all before it. Feeling cold at Deauville and putting on a jockey's sweater, she started another fashion. Her soft unsensational silk blouses toned down over-emphasis; she dressed women in short skirts for the first time. She thought life must be the race-course of her dreams.

All impediments gave way before her youthful ardour. 'My hair was crushing me to death,' she said. 'One evening I was going to the Opera with an elderly Greek, and dressing, with my maid, in my little apartment in the avenue Gabriel – I'd never been to the Opera before. I had a white dress made by my own modistes. My hair, which came down below my waist, was done up round my head in three braids – all that mass set straight on top of that thin body. I couldn't dress at Cheruit's, I couldn't wear anything – I was all muscles, so those grosgrains . . . I looked like a little Greek with my smooth braids. There was a gas burner in the bathroom. I turned on the hot tap to wash my hands again, the water wasn't hot, so I fiddled with the pilot-light and the whole thing exploded. My white dress was covered in soot, my hair – the less said the better. I only had to wash my face again – I didn't use make-up. In those days only the cocottes used make-up and were elegant. The women of the bourgeoisie weren't groomed – and they wore hats that flopped all over the place, with birds' nests and butterflies.

'I took a pair of scissors and cut one braid off. The hair sprang out at once all round my face. In those days I had hair like sable. I must cut off the others, I thought. I wanted to go to the Opera, you see!

'When I called the maid to cut off the third braid she started to cry. I told her the cook wouldn't be able to hear the door-bell – I had two Basque girls, sisters – when Monsieur Nicolopoulo rang. I slipped on a black dress I had, crossed over in front – what a marvellous thing, youth – and caught in at the waist, with a sort of minaret on top.

' "Monsieur Poulo, Monsieur Poulo, Mademoiselle is five minutes late, but she'll be ready right away – she had a little spot on her dress." '

They made a dazzling entrance at the Opera. That day Coco, the darling of the English, became the beauty of Paris. 'Do you see that neck, that woman – who is she?' 'Who are they talking about?' Coco asked Nicolopoulo. 'You, of course. I'm so proud.' 'I cut off my hair.' 'Did you really?' said Nicolo-poulo, who hadn't noticed anything.

'When I got back that evening they'd washed my hair and my braids were waiting for me in the bathroom like three dead bodies . . . Ever since, during the collections, I've always plied the scissors,' she said, tugging at her fringe.

Another decisive cut was to mark her life, so that no other hands could ever join it together in its first slim flame. Boy Capel and Coco, separated by the war, met again afterwards. He was passionately fond of India and arranged for two Indians to join the polo teams. She was fascinated by their marvellous eyes and their turbans. The carnal only reinforced the appeal, deeper in her, of the invisible and spiritual. Boy, the theosophist, believed in a life after death. 'Nothing dies, not even a grain of sand, so nothing is lost – I like that very much,' she said. This pledge from beyond was to bind them together through the absolute separation to come. Boy Capel was killed in a motoring accident.

Six months after his death, one of the Indians came to see her and told her she must begin to live again for his sake. The precious cargo of mourning she confided to no one. Her favourite novel was Emily Brontë's: in her view, no film ever succeeded in portraying its characters. It tells of an imperishable love, on wild moors swept by a storm she knew well. Only *Wuthering Heights* heard her lament. Much later, she told me: 'I've wept so much. Now I don't cry any more. When you don't cry it's because you don't believe in happiness any more.'

She took refuge on the Côte d'Azur where, breathing in essences and fields of Bulgarian roses, she invented the perfume – Number 5 – which was to obsess the world. The name was a chance, not premeditated: she called it that because it was the fifth bottle and five is a pretty number. With a wave of the hand she annihilated the hideous Lalique flagons with fancy stoppers, meant to be kept, and invented the plain throw-away bottle marked with a neat black figure, servant of the most exclusive sense, the sense of smell. Paul Valéry's aphorism became her motto: 'A woman who doesn't use perfume has no future.' Her perfume was her instinct, her unconstraint. The smell of burnt sandalwood, Russian leather, gardenia and jasmin spread her fable. That most indefinable of secrets, that which a woman is steeped in and which lingers behind her, was to go with her day and night. 'Women wear the perfumes they're given as presents. You ought to wear your own, the one you like. If I leave a jacket behind somewhere, they know it's mine. When I was young, the first thing I'd have done if I had any money was buy some perfume. I'd been given Floris's Sweet Peas . . . I thought it was lovely, country girl that I was. Then I realised it didn't suit me. Apollinaire, Marie Laurencin's lover, smelt awful!'

The senses stumbled on souvenir. For Coco the artistic world was a new world in which she always kept the ardour of an immigrant. Up till then she'd known only austere Protestants and the upper middle classes: this was a revelation.

It all began with a dinner party at Cécile Sorel's which Albert Flament had arranged for her one day because that was what 'seemed to me the most splendid thing possible.' What a disappointment! 'I found everything was false.' She'd been told the table was gold, and all she saw was an unattractive gilt cloth with fruit scattered about all over it. 'Horrible! A plain white cloth is at least clean.' Moth-eaten scraps of old panther hung at the windows. 'I learned to see what was ugly.' There were mirrors on the floor: Ségur, Cécile's husband, said to her, 'Whatever time I get home, my dear, drunk, exhausted or asleep, I can never imagine it's a lake.' Cécile, who had false teeth, thrust her dentures so near her young guest they looked as if they were going to fall out. 'My pigeon,' she called her. Coco sat next to José Maria Sert, the painter.

'What a beautiful voice you have, Madame.'

'But I'm not married.'

'You soon will be.'

A pianist played funeral marches; she asked for a record on the gramophone. After dinner she was seized by a woman with a little chignon whom she took to be Sert's wife, and who in fact was to become so. This was Misia. 'Two vultures swooped down on the little pigeon,' said Cécile Sorel, 'and wouldn't let go of her.'

'A few days later Misia arrived at my place at nine in the morning. My servants hated her – every single morning she came and woke me up. "Come along, darling, we're going to see Sarah Bernhardt." "But I saw her when I was thirteen

Misia Sert. Portrait by Bonnard

and cried my eyes out." "No, no, quick – we're going to see her on her death-bed."

'It was terrible – they were queuing up. Sarah was dead, and all I saw was a poor little lifeless ruin with a scrap of tulle, holding a bunch of violets. Louise Abbéma was weeping silently in a cape and a three-cornered hat. I didn't know whether Sarah Bernhardt was those little remains or her. Sarah's son was in a hideous modernistic middle-class dining-room with a light hanging down from the ceiling. "What on earth's the matter with you?" Misia asked. I was pale as death. The sordidness of it all . . . It took that to show me the provinces had a certain elegance.'

When Boy Capel died there were about twenty other

José Maria Sert, Misia (centre) and Germaine Sorel, Réjane's daughter, at Deauville

Englishmen waiting to marry her. She met Dimitri of Russia at the Ritz. His father had just been murdered and his sister, instead of being queen of Sweden, was selling her jewellery. 'I've got a new car,' Coco said to him. 'Would you like to come with me to Monte Carlo to try it out?' 'I haven't much money.' 'That doesn't matter – the mechanic will pay for the petrol and we don't need to stay in the most expensive hotel.' The manager of the hotel, she recalled nostalgically, didn't want to give Dimitri a bill. ' "Oh yes, you must," I told him. "Just a little one." '

The papers announced that Coco was marrying the Grand Duke, and Misia, with Polish malice, said the midinette had

Misia, while she was still Mrs Edwards, on board her yacht.
On the left, in straw hat, Sem

run off with a Russian prince. The Grand Duke Michael came
to see her to say he'd dreamed the Czar said Coco and Dimitri
must marry, it was their destiny. Coco answered the Czar hadn't
come and told *her*. 'Those Grand Dukes were all the same –
they looked marvellous but there was nothing behind. Green
eyes, fine hands and shoulders, peace-loving, timorous. They
drank so as not to be afraid. They were tall and handsome and
splendid, but behind it all –nothing: just vodka and the void.'
She told Dimitri, 'Don't cry, I won't be your wife and I'll never
be your mistress. No one was asking you to sleep on the floor.'
Meanwhile Misia wired to Igor Stravinsky, who was madly
in love with Coco, while she herself, unaware of all this,
cabled to Barcelona that she was coming to attend his concert.

Her commonsense saw through Misia. 'She was the first
card I played,' she told me one day. Misia was the daughter
of a Polish Jewish sculptor whose plaster casts of female

nudes stood in the niches of the casino at Monte Carlo. When she came into a drawing-room everyone said, 'Here comes Mother Menace.' Erik Satie would say, 'Still, a fine cat.' 'Yes,' came the answer, 'but keep the birds out of the way.' Misia had a passion for catastrophes and for people. Disaster was meat and drink to her. She'd provoke it, stage-manage it, and when it collapsed round her ears she'd provoke another. She was not 'received' in society. Coco, fêted everywhere and surrounded by Englishmen all vying for her, didn't know what this was. 'I'd read so many novels, nothing in life ever surprised me. I couldn't be a snob – I'd lived among them since the age of six.'

But Coco's shyness was incomprehensible to Misia. 'She always used to say the thing she liked best was watching me come into a drawing-room. My heart used to sink into my boots. But Misia had the cheek of the devil and liked nothing better than to go where she wasn't invited. I'd have died rather!' Society soon bored her. Whereas 'Misia and Sert, they were loads of bad taste, but – Constantinople!' And she added drolly, 'I hadn't yet got my feet on the ground.' She landed in the middle of the Russian ballet. 'I missed the provinces so! When I met the Russians . . .' An invisible magnet drew her. She adored *Thamar*, the designs of Bakst, and *Schéhérazade*. 'It was very theatrical, it took you right out of yourself.' That was her quest. 'It was when I saw the Diaghilev ballet I decided I was going to live in what I loved.' She went to all the rehearsals, where she saw Picasso and Stravinsky. Picasso – 'a Spaniard, with his hat' – fixed her with his coal-black eyes. Misia told her she'd saved her from Picasso. By what right? asked Coco. 'I regarded him as a clown. But his black eyes petrified me. I turned round, and was furious with myself for doing it. He disturbed me.' One day Picasso was to tell her there were two kinds of woman, goddesses and mattresses. Coco remained a goddess. At the ballet too she saw Massine, very handsome, and indecently thin; Bakst, comic and enormous; Chirico, always ill. 'You got the impression there was nothing but illness . . . Cocteau fastened on to all these people in the hope some talent would rub off on him. First of all he followed the Rostands, then he got to know Picasso.' His best works, in her opinion, were his caricatures – copied from Sem though, she added briskly. She could already detect sham.

In those conventional times it was a revelation. The balloon was punctured. She made the Chinaman's costume for Diaghilev – speaking of him, her eyes filled with dream, fear, memory. He taught her all about escape and breaking bounds. Just before one of her collections she dumbfounded her work-people by recalling how Diaghilev, after a morning's rehearsal said to the orchestra: 'You love your profession, don't you, messieurs?' They squirmed a little, but the rehearsals went on and lasted till five o'clock. Then Diaghilev put on his threadbare pelisse. It was impossible to get him to wear a new one. 'No, really – think of my dancers, my company . . .' Finally she ordered one for him. He sold it before it was delivered. Coco was furious for half an hour, then yielded to his arguments. 'He was right.'

For her, Diaghilev represented intelligence. He sent Serge Lifar to Milan to 'work' with Petipa, the ballet-master, and posted him parcels of books. 'Serge had just left the conservatoire, all he knew anything about was music, he'd started out literally on foot . . . and he was untutored here,' she said, pointing to her brow. 'Dancing is not dancing in front of a mirror. You have to forget that.' The thick woollen tights live again, against the unique leaps of Nijinski, greasepaint melting on a face consumed by effort, and the revelation of the fallen mask: *The Spectre of the Rose, The Firebird.* 'It's very tiring having to throw ballerinas back and forth, you know. At first you just dance, no problem, but dancing's not a pair of points and a phiz. I've seen plenty of dancers and you have to dance with this' – touching her solar plexus swiftly and letting her hand fly off – 'and then away.' As for a dancer's physique, to be attractive on the stage he needs a Russian face, slightly twisted. 'You're born with genius. Talent has to be brought out.'

All her senses warned her: the strength of an element that is imprisoned escapes. In her room at the Ritz she leafed through the catalogue of the Russian Ballet exhibition in Strasbourg. In the preface Serge Lifar mentioned the square named after Diaghilev. 'Obstinate as a mule,' she said, meaning Lifar. 'Place Diaghilev! A little pocket handkerchief in front of the Galeries Lafayette. Very Russian, the way they always manage to make their point . . . Burn some incense paper,' she told her maid, Céline. 'I do that every day – it's my East,' she explained in one of her sudden returns to the everyday, which she wouldn't abandon for anything.

She loved that which was foreign, which carried her away, far away, from the sedentary bourgeoisie. The Mdivani brothers were savages from Tiflis. 'They were impossibly handsome and used to ride into drawing-rooms on horse-back, roaring with laughter.' The prophetic tribe with glowing eyes, beloved of Baudelaire, had recognised a kindred spirit. 'They were Caucasians, Orientals. They dreamed of living close to nature, with big fires at night, and wanted to take me away with their sister, Roussy. Dimitri, the grand duke of Russia, told me their father was general of the Czar's guard.' Sert decreed there should be no formal dress at Deauville: they got themselves up to the nines and wore three carnations in their buttonhole. All they wanted was to get Roussy back – she was so like her brothers she had to wear a ribbon to distinguish her when they wrestled. They went about everywhere accompanied by the bodies of their mother and father in a lead coffin, to take back to the Caucasus: Misia had them buried in Père Lachaise. They all made wealthy marriages in California – they smelt the oil as they came out of the water. Everyone adored them. One of the brothers married Barbara Hutton.

Coco followed the errant fancies of Misia and Sert, and went

'Her solitude was soon to be lit up'

with them to Venice. On the Lido they had to pass the cabin belonging to the Princess San Faustino, mother of Madame Agnelli. 'She was dressed all in white, with white hair. She frightened me.

' "Well, child, what are you looking for here?"

' "Nothing, Madame."

' "But you are. All women look for love. Here people are always talking about it but never make it." '

Misia was actually Mrs Edwards, and what was Coco's amazement, on their first Venetian journey, when she came to call for her in the morning and found Sert in her bed, unshaven and in black pyjamas. He was a hirsute Catalan of whom Bérard said, 'When he comes out of the shower he has a sort of fur pelt.' Misia was neither a cocotte nor a lady. She probably dreamed of becoming a cocotte, a kept woman, when she married Edwards. When she woke up she used to rub her cheeks with a dab of rouge and a doe's-foot: 'I don't want to look miserable all day long . . .' Coco never forgot that lesson. Was she at that time the silent black swan Cocteau speaks of, which she recognised as 'the thing most like me' in a swift caricature by Sem? The chiaroscuro of her solitude was soon to be lit up: she met the man who was to be her life's companion for fourteen years – the Duke of Westminster.

'I'm not one of those women who belong to several men. I'm sure it was Boy who sent Westminster to me.' With her the story of tenderness and passion would always be accompanied by a nostalgia for death. Only one person could have made her animally happy. He was gone. The primitive mistrust and disconcerting feminine resistance which derived deep down

The Duke of Westminster

from her lonely childhood and the loss of her first love were never to leave her.

Coco met the Duke of Westminster at Monte Carlo at Christmas. She was invited, with Vera Lombardi Bates, to dine on his yacht. They went dancing. They were to meet again at Easter. 'Till then I didn't want to hear anything about him: I just got on with my job in the rue Cambon.'

He owned vast hothouses, and every day his footman came with England's first crocuses and primroses, and a letter. 'Men used to woo and be tender,' she said, musing. 'Tenderness – that's what the world hasn't got any more.' She recalled the dinner given by the Polignacs for the Prince of Wales, at Henri's in the place Gaillon the day before Good Friday. 'Melchior de Polignac was fond of his champagne. I didn't know it was all business.' The Prince of Wales conveyed that he would like to have a drink at her place. 'Before would be better than too late. May I come at six?' 'That will be perfect, your highness.' 'Call me David.'

The Prince drank two cocktails and Coco said she must go and change. 'How long will it take?' 'An hour and a half – I have to do you justice, and I mustn't arrive after you do.' He promised his car wouldn't appear until after hers. She wore a dress of white muslin, and when she got there Vera Lombardi rushed up saying she was late. 'But the Prince of Wales isn't here yet, is he?' He came in – and put Coco on his right, made her smoke through his cigarette-holder, and rose from the table because she was getting bored. General Trotter, delighted that his prince was enjoying himself, organised the cars. They went to a night-club and danced. Coco was in good spirits because she was soon going to see the Duke of Westminster again for the first time since Christmas. It got late, she didn't want to eat meat, the Prince summoned the Negress to cook her little *crêpes*. She'd rather have gone home to bed.

She'd arranged to meet Westminster three days later on his yacht at Bayonne. It was a honeymoon voyage.

38

'Out of my three chaps, the Prince of Wales, Dimitri of Russia, and the Duke of Westminster, I chose the one who protected me best.' She described the man whose wealth eclipsed everyone else's as 'the simplest person in the world. With him I saw the acme of riches and rarity. But he didn't know the meaning of the word snobbery. It would never have occurred to him. He was simplicity itself, simple as a tramp.'

He was called Bendor, Ben or Benny, after Bendor, his father's famous stallion: he too was tall and fair. 'It was the Westminsters who were the rightful kings. The others were usurpers, Normans.' He'd given jobs to all his school friends: one looked after the horses, the other the game preserves, another Scotland, another the yachts. His enormous fortune was almost an encumbrance, and his one preoccupation was not to be noticed and to do as he liked.

'In the rue Cambon on February 5 and August 5, the days of my collection, the tiger paced up and down. I was leaving that evening.' The Duke of Westminster's house was more like a cathedral than a house: he called it St Pancras Station. It was built in the Gothic style, at once hideous and magnificent. 'If you raised your eyes you saw a man and a woman by Goya. You sat on the Order of the Garter. '*Honi soit qui mal y pense*' was embroidered on all the chairs. There was a manservant behind each chair, and warriors in armour on every stair. But they must have been very small – I tried, in riding breeches, to get into several suits and they were all too tight. I had a good laugh one day: I told Westminster the Englishwomen made love to the footmen at night and in the daytime they were all too well-bred to recognise one another. Englishwomen are the maddest and most unpredictable women I know. If the footmen were good-looking they would go, all innocence, for a week-end, but pretend not to know their night-time lovers. *I* would have thrown my arms round my lover's neck! When you do a servant the honour of sleeping with him, he becomes the master.'

The Duke of Westminster

Coco aboard *Flying Cloud*

But what Englishwomen do you really know?' the Duke answered. 'All that's only what the French say.'

One evening he had a secret meeting with his lawyer to discuss his divorce. No one was supposed to know about it except Coco. There was a dinner-party, followed by a ball. At one o'clock he disappeared, but when he came out of the room where the interview with the lawyer had taken place he heard a noise in the corridor and hid behind a suit of armour. He saw a shadow slip by and start to go into the room of one of the young ladies staying in the house. He tackled the man and found it was Murphy, his valet, who'd been with him thirty-eight years. 'Excuse me,' he said.

He called him the Jesuit. 'Why?' asked Coco.

'Because he's a Catholic. All Catholics are Jesuits.'

The Rolls-Royces were changed every year, but only the engines. The body was kept as it was. To have a new car was inexcusable extravagance. 'We're not Argentinians,' said the Duke. Coco's maid told her he only handed his shoes on to his valet when they couldn't be mended any more. The Duke liked Coco's maid: she saw to his shoes for him – his valet was ashamed to have them re-soled for the umpteenth time. 'The uppers are all worn out,' he'd say. What was that to the Duke, who loved dancing: it was night, artificial light, and they were black. He only liked shoes with holes in them. They were comfortable, and he didn't want any others. Coco ordered him a dozen pairs at Bunting's without telling him, and had put them in his wardrobe.

Hiding behind a bush in the grounds, waterlogged with the recent rain, she saw the Duke in a new pair of shoes, whistling, his hands in his trouser pockets, go up to a big puddle and jump into it to take the shine off them.

One day she was walking along the Canebière in Marseilles with the Duke when his hat got dusty and he went into a shop to have it brushed. 'It's very old,' said the man, who must have been the proprietor, as the Duke left a tip. 'The

Duke was furious,' laughed Coco. 'That old hat was the apple of his eye.'

The sea, the realm of wrinkles, bored the young woman and made her sad. She couldn't swim. 'Pass me your binoculars,' she used to say, 'so I can see if there's anything to see.' Alas, there was nothing but the crew of forty-five standing to attention. The only consolation was the discipline. 'You didn't have to ring twice.' She noticed that on the yacht 'white and navy-blue are the only possible colours. The Navy's colours. And it's not by accident they wear black ties: they're all in mourning for Nelson.' She liked the white watches on the tanned wrists. 'I can't bear those little things from Cartier's that cost a fortune.' When *Flying Cloud* was out at sea, Coco had a presentiment and made them turn back to Venice. Diaghilev, shivering in his dinner-jacket, the only warm garment he had left, was dying.

She never lost her spirit of independence. 'At the end of a year I gave back a bookful of blank cheques to the man who loved me, and said, "Here, I've used the money I earned myself." His secretary protested in vain: "But all the Duchesses..."

When Mary, the Duke of Westminster's daughter, had her coming-out ball, she invited Mademoiselle Chanel. This pleased her father so much he gave her the present he knew would delight her most: four horses. That evening Coco gave an enchanting dinner-party in David Street, inviting the Duchess of Westminster, who came, her daughters, the Duke, Kutuzov, Winston Churchill, and a few friends. When it was time to leave for the ball she said gaily they couldn't all arrive *en famille*, and she'd come on later. The Duke promised to have a table ready for her where she wouldn't be bored. He hadn't been waiting a quarter of an hour when he got anxious and sent Kutuzov to fetch her: she sent a message that she was changing her dress. 'That doesn't sound at all like her,' said the Duke. 'And she had a marvellous white dress on already.' But it was a question of window-dressing. Queen

Mary had said of Coco that she was not the sort of person to submit to all the old lorgnettes in London.

She'd covered her face with cream and dusted it with talc, put black mascara under her eyes, and huddled in bed with a hot-water-bottle which she kept as close to her as she could to try to induce a temperature. When Kutuzov told the Duke she wasn't well and wouldn't be coming, he at once left the ball and rushed to her room. 'What's wrong? Have you seen a doctor?' he cried on seeing all this production. Then she rubbed her face gently against his shoulder: he saw his jacket go white and understood, and smiled. 'You see,' she said. 'In the first place I don't like doing things that bore me. And in the second, you wouldn't really have liked it either.' All London had been betting on it: would she come or wouldn't she? But the rebel had eluded them.

The Duchess, charmed, sent to inquire after her and offered to come during the night. A message was sent saying it wasn't really necessary.

But neither the river Tweed nor the Scottish streams captivated Coco. Misia, now Madame Sert, felt like a fish out of water in Scotland. One day she wanted to go to the post. Coco told her it was twenty miles away and asked if she could ride a horse. During the day there were fishing expeditions in which Winston Churchill, tongue to the fore, caught nothing; in the evening, Chinese bezique. Coco could still remember the salmon struggling fiercely against death. An expert fisherman who was fond of her told her not to bother too much about the sky or the colour of the water: use a black doctor fly if it's cloudy and a silver doctor if it's fine. She preferred picnics, setting off with great hampers, seeing gipsy women smoking pipes. 'I lived at a place near Chester, where the prizes at the cattle shows were cheeses the size of this table.' One day the head gardener told Percy Smith, the steward, that the hothouse had been raided. The Duke cut the accusation short: Coco was the burglar. They'd been going through the hothouses and Coco, who didn't like hothouses, had eaten the Christmas strawberries and introduced the Duke to the nectarines of her childhood.

Pink coats, collars and cuffs the colour of a Child of Mary, pheasants falling like rain to a chorus of 'Mine!' One evening when there was a hunt dinner, Coco went to the hothouses and cut all the azaleas: she arranged a gold table between the crimson of the windows and all the shades of brown and russet flowers. 'The only way not to hate azaleas,' she said to me, 'is to cut them.' 'I wish I knew the swine who did that,' growled the English lord who took her in to dinner. 'You're arm in arm with him,' she said.

Westminster, out of his mind with delight, thought she was going to marry him. She kept putting it off till next year. Sometimes the Duke drank, and he told Coco he hadn't had the education of a duke. She looked at him warily as he drank: she'd threatened, if he had another glass, to get up and kiss him on the lips. 'I'm French – what do I care? *I'm* not English!'

Every day she went to see the Duke's mother, who lived a few miles away across the estate. 'Darling, marry Benny,' the old lady used to say to her. 'The first years are the best.' But Coco told Westminster she'd get married only if she was expecting a child – 'That was my blackmail, you see.' 'In that case,' she told him, 'I'd be very pleased to get married. But otherwise what's the point? People can stop loving one another, and then all the doors are shut. Marriage . . . one marries for security, prestige. I'm not interested in all that.' When Westminster showed her the big cedar tree where he meant to be buried, together with all the dogs he'd ever had since he was five years old, 'Nonsense,' she told him – he'd be buried in the cathedral paved with his ancestors' tombs.

One stormy night three thousand trees were blown down and nobody noticed. Coco went for a five-hour ride and thought she'd been over the whole estate. She'd seen only a third of it. 'I came away without looking at the rest.' Uninhabited woods bored her. There were very few animals.

'I've never fired a gun . . . but I have puffed on a pipe! I'd seen everything, understood everything. I tried playing tennis – I was bored to death. The empty golf course' – she went there on Sunday, the day reserved for the servants – 'the hot-houses where they burned coal from their own mines, grapes in February, peaches in January . . .'

But she never forgot the lifesize horse in the Westminster stables – 'it'll be there till it crumbles to dust'; her friendship with a dog that used to go with her to the races; her box upholstered in navy-blue, left empty. 'Mademoiselle Chanel's house is still there in David Street,' she told me on the last day of her life. She always remained close to the rides through the forest leading to the sea, the thoroughbreds that pranced and then were quiet, boar-hunts where the quarry suddenly emerged on to the beach. 'At Mimizan, when the boar had been killed, there was a delicious smell: the scent of tuberoses growing on sand.' She went to savour it by the lair of the female and her young: the cook told her it was the smell of the boar in love. 'It's with the male sexual organs, not the female, that the best perfumes are made. Vibrant, full of life.' The season of love . . . Mimizan and its heaths was also the memory of her accident.

'There were still men walking on stilts and knitting great thick woollen stockings.' She was in riding-habit, with a hat and a spotted veil covering her face. One of the hunting party let a branch spring back on her, splitting open her upper lip. Her face was covered in blood, her white stock spattered, the Duke shouted, 'Who was the idiot who did that?' He had the huntsman blow his horn and stop the hunt. The doctor came rushing: a vet, who sewed her up with pig's bristle. 'His thread was too thick – provincial.' Coco took the train, wept in the wagon-lit, had her first breakdown. The last straw was that the previous day she'd bought a monkey and a parrot: they screeched and yelled at one another in some mysterious language – 'Brazilian, I think.' The monkey clung to her skirt, and her maid couldn't manage to cover up the now

Coco's apartment in the Faubourg Saint-Honoré

hysterical parrot's cage to keep it quiet. Her pets would be made of gilt in future.

She was expected in the Faubourg Saint-Honoré, where she'd taken an apartment in the hôtel de Lauzun. Mathilde de Rothschild called hallo through the window: she'd said of Coco, holding up her little fingernail, 'I shan't buy that much without showing her. That child's got more taste than the rest put together.' The Rothschilds had a lot of jewellery dating from the Third Republic, and Mathilde took her with her to Cartier's where she wanted to have some of it re-set. 'Too small,' said Coco. 'Slender, perhaps?' suggested the assistant. 'Jewellery isn't meant to be skimpy,' she answered.

Coco created fairyland in her huge salon which she made look smaller with mirrors and two grand pianos: her childhood dream, with couches and great tall blackamoors carrying shells. Composers, dancers, artists met there. 'Music. People lay on settees and I discovered art.' The time was long past when Misia, eearing her play Gounod's *Ave Maria* on the piano, exclaimed, 'My dear child, what dreadful stuff!' 'But Misia,' said Coco, 'the song and the words are by Gounod and the prelude's by Bach.' The black swan had spread its wings, and taken in the revival of Stravinsky's *Rite of Spring* and Satie's *Parade*. 'With those people you were never bored. They didn't talk art, thank God, they created it, which isn't the same thing.' Not allowed to go and see Radiguet when he was dying of typhus, Coco arranged for him to be taken to a nursing home in the rue Puccini with a cool clean bed; organised his funeral, as between artists, and sent masses of flowers. No one thanked her for footing the bill. They thanked Madame Sert, who said to her, 'Why do you do all this?'

'I used to give two or three dances a year, and dinner parties. Never a big formal table. Waiters to serve, but always a cold buffet. One can live without servants. I'd lived in England, hadn't I! The English breakfast – at Westminster's there was cold meat and porridge ready at any hour of the day or night. You need drink for the guests and for the music. They used to stay at my place till nine in the morning, and had to be told to go out through the garden, the way they'd come in.' At the 'Ambassadors' Coco had discovered forty-five black musicians; she had them come at midnight, after a French band had played waltzes and an Argentine band tangos. One evening when she was giving a dance Misia found her asleep on the settee in the salon. 'What! Not ready? Have you cancelled the dance?' 'No, but there were things I wasn't satisfied with so I changed the lights.' 'What a marvellous smell!' exclaimed Misia. 'Yes, I've seen to that.' Perfume was burning in every room.

What fascinated her guests most was her bedroom, hung with mirrors. 'I want to see what she sleeps in,' said Maurice de Rothschild, giving a large tip to her maid. The bed was made, the room deserted, but on turning back the cover he found sheets of – white cotton.

The sideboards at Etienne de Beaumont's were always empty. 'Nothing but water or cloudy lemonade.' She hired the Pleyel bar for him one evening. She could still recall the black dinner-jacket Picasso had had made for himself. The others all told him how splendid he looked. 'But he'd already had enough of it. It was Olga who wanted to mix in society – anyway, he left her. If he dresses badly nowadays it's on purpose, to forget the dinner-jacket he wore once or twice to go to the Beaumonts'' – the tall Etienne de Beaumont and his wife Edith who was satisfied with everything. 'The one thing the Beaumonts wanted to avoid was being "old hat". They had an enormous organ in their salon, covered with a theatre curtain, and above it they hung a Picasso.' Marie Laurencin lived in a little house in their garden. 'She was the equivalent of Françoise Hardy nowadays – right on the borderline. It was all on a small scale, but it was a whole circle in which you discovered art with a capital A.'

Coco laughed, remembering a dance there to which she went dressed as a sailor, with a black face and wearing a

Lunch at La Pausa

uniform belonging to 'No Luck', Cocteau's sailor friend. Etienne de Beaumont wanted her to go in a bathing suit, with sandals to make her taller. 'He liked giantesses, but I was so shy . . .' In her opinion her host was too fond of giving orders, but he had some very fine pictures. 'His boast was that he never paid for one of them!' He'd quarrelled with Diaghilev and composed a ballet to annoy him – 'It didn't annoy him at all. How could a man-about-town, however much cheek he had, compete? I didn't go to see it – I didn't want to hurt Diaghilev's feelings. Talent is what I respect above everything.' She went on to tell how one day the Duke of Westminster told Beaumont he looked as if he was born to be guillotined.

Coco had decided: she was not going to be a duchess in London. She found a wife for Westminster, who turned up two days after the wedding. 'What a mess we've made of it,' he said. He escorted her back from the Lotti, the hotel he'd been staying in since he was three, to the Faubourg Saint-

Coco sitting on the branch of an olive tree at La Pausa

Honoré, smoking a cigar. 'Loelia went through with it because of you. Otherwise . . .' 'The porter looked at me in amazement as I went by, crying. Loelia – Loelia, whom I'd made him marry, was embroidering blue roses!'

Coco packed her bags and left her private house in the Faubourg, installing herself at the Ritz in the place Vendôme, from which she emigrated during the Occupation to the rue Cambon, just a few yards away from her fashion house. 'In a hotel, I feel I'm travelling.' At La Pausa, her marvellous house in the south of Roquebrune, the proud convent gates rose up in the walls of summer. The seamless carpets, all alike in fawn and brown, came from Spain; the divans were wide enough to sleep on, shaded by Venetian ochre curtains. 'As soon as you lay down, bronze cushions went the colour of the books blending into the shelves.' What she liked at Roquebrune was the cool dark of the vestibule, and breathing her house full of flowers. Tuberoses sprang forward, lavender and irises climbed over the patio. 'A tree grew inside the house.

We lived underneath it.' If someone annoyed her she would have lunch outside under the olive-tree. No servants until you rang for coffee. A photograph shows her sitting on a branch of the olive-tree, smiling, in wide trousers. She liked to have mosquito-nets in the bedrooms, draped at the sides and tucked in. Like that one was 'protected'. The shutters were of natural wood, the furniture of her room simple and unpainted. Under her balcony, while taking her siesta, she heard the compliment that gave her greatest pleasure. Foucault de la Verdura, showing the house to a visitor, cried, 'What genius to have spent all that money so that it doesn't show!'

Love had not yet deserted her path. The designer Paul Iribe was often her guest at La Pausa. He told her he'd like to die there: and coming towards her on the tennis-court he fell dead of a stroke.

Coco left La Pausa. No house was able to hold her. She didn't stay long at Mesnil-Guillaume, nine hundred acres near Lisieux. 'What was I supposed to do with cows? In the first place I've never liked animals with horns. I've always fled that sort of place . . . In that case it was because they'd taken away the fireplaces and installed central heating.' Live fires have charm for nomads.

A month in Italy every year. The Serts were fond of food and went to bed early. 'During the day they showed me all there was to see, and in the evening I joined the riff-raff. I liked the day to end – its twilight and my anguish. One doesn't go to Italy for gentlemen – I always paid.'

One day at Capri, at Mona Williams's, she and Misia and Luchino Visconti and Roussy were riding and laughing on donkeys. It was two o'clock, but everyone was still on the beach. 'I was afraid of being late. My donkey fell, with me still astride, and Roussy told me my white pants were dirty – she knew I couldn't stand that. I laughed, then I saw Williams's face watching us, with such sadness I knew something was wrong.

Coco's house at Mesnil-Guillaume, Normandy

'Williams – that's the sort of American I like. He'd made his money himself. He was a worker – he'd been a tram-driver. He was the most distinguished man I know.' At lunch he asked her if she'd go away with him that afternoon. "Mona's a mannequin, just a mannequin. Come with me." But Coco answered, "My dear, it's too late."

'Perhaps a year earlier I'd have gone with him. He had a yacht, and that's the best thing for running away to start a love affair. The first time you're clumsy, the second you quarrel a bit, and if it doesn't go well, the third time you can stop at a port.' But it was too late. 'We were at his wife's house, and Westminster was still alive.' But she was to tell me, 'The only thing I regret is not having gone away with Williams.' The intensity of his sadness had made her heart beat faster.

'I've always had the courage to go away, and if I haven't had the courage I've been helped by providence, by death . . . A woman hasn't all that many ways of defending herself. She has to go.'

Work

The artistic temperament cannot bear vagueness.
OSCAR WILDE

Work

Yet between truant furies Coco did cast anchor somewhere, in a Chinese garden, a house of mirrors: 81 rue Cambon. 'I have one white being and one black,' she used to say to me. 'Like Rubens's superb "Four Negroes".' Her passion for liberty yielded before something more primitive, closer to the marvellous: workmanship.

Anyone who didn't see Chanel bent to her task like an insect seeking its pollen, searching, scrutinising, fertilising, has missed the essential part of her being. Something inexpressible in her took over and carried her away, plunged in her true element. When she stopped, all that was left of another conquered day was a fatigue without happiness. So against whom did she measure herself in her work? Against the secret public of her own childhood, the little private abyss which had left its unfathomable mark on her, even though that trace now extended to the world, society. Her desperate alter ego, the lonely child, was always in danger. She never ceased to cover, and discover, her own want.

She subtracted. Coco Chanel couldn't sew. She cut. 'All you have to do is subtract. They bring you length and width. What you have to do is cut.' Madame Raymonde hung a long white tape round her neck with her special collection scissors threaded on it. This strange necklace was part of the rite. Her precious Coromandel tables were laden with silver-gilt scissors and plain ones from Nogent. Her tools were everywhere: in rows on her dressing-table at the Ritz, even spread out on a white napkin on her bedside table. One day when she was showing me her English gold boxes, decked with the arms of generations, she said: 'You see, when they come into a family that family adds its own marks. I would add my scissors.'

They represented an indispensable order – perhaps, more irresistibly still, her destiny, which she never satisfied. In the first years of the century she opened her shop in Deauville; she opened in the rue Cambon in 1914, and almost believed the war broke out to spite her. When the armistice finally came, and the mad twenties, Chanel opened to women the way to liberty and independence. 'It was the Russians who taught women it isn't degrading to work. My grand duchesses used to knit.' Women had changed during the war. Left to themselves, they'd got thinner, learned to do without corsets and lady's maids. Chanel believed in her own luck: 'My time was ready for me, waiting – all I had to do was come on the scene.' Just as Kandinsky revealed modern art by a painting hung upside down, so she stripped convention and disgraced emphatic elegance. 'Who wants to carry his money round his neck?' She had her pearls copied; she reinvented jewellery. In 1922 she disembarked at Cannes from the finest yacht in the world, and her sunburn made tan no longer taboo. 'What made you launch the fashion for trousers?' a journalist asked her. 'Strange as it may seem, modesty.' She couldn't bear seeing people lunching on the Lido in Venice in wet swimsuits: 'They stick to you – it's not decent.' What had become of Boldini's Americans strangled with pearls? She wore her legendary ones over a sweater.

Chanel No. 5 emanated from simple bottles. According to Chanel the sense of smell is the only one that is still instinctive. It lives on nostalgia, the subconscious. 'Leading them by the nose,' she wrote in London. 'It's something very special. It mustn't stain, it has to smell very good – otherwise it's a flop, cheap bazaar stuff.' She couldn't be fooled. Her defences scented out jasmin, Russian leather, Bulgarian roses, Tonkin musk, the smell of a magnolia unfolding its petals. When it begins to rot it smells of mushrooms. That was her discovery. And to the angry and intransigent scent of lilies or tuberoses

'She wore her legendary pearls over a sweater'

she linked the mushroom: 'It smells of grass and humus, something fresh and cool, You have to lessen the intensity of tuberoses. Otherwise it's like this,' she said, sampling the perfume her chemist had brought her. 'It lacks the whiff that makes you remember.' The chemist returned to the salon with a little bottle in his waistcoat pocket. 'You've discovered the mushroom!' she said as soon as he set foot through the door. 'What a nose,' he answered.

'It was she who launched the things we like now.' Coco in 1928

It was she who launched the things we like now – the once despised jersey, the little black dress, beige, navy blue and white, real pockets, comfortable coats, bell-bottomed trousers and artificial jewellery. It was a revolution that takes us through nearly half a century in which her muslins, her scissors, reigned over feminine mystery. Her first dresses were made in a single workshop. The fashion house in the rue Cambon soon occupied five buildings and employed three thousand work-girls. Elsa Schiaparelli arrived with exuberant enthusiasm from Italy and launched shocking pink, coats lined with variegated rabbit's fur, the circus groom's jacket and the clown's hat. Her theatrical baroque toppled over into surrealism. 'I only like primitives,' said Chanel. 'The rest is just wallpaper.' Stravinsky, Picasso, Bérard and Cocteau watched her models file down her mirror-lined stairs.

In 1939 she vanished into Switzerland and the south of France and abandoned haute couture. 'No one thinks of making beautiful clothes when there's a war on.' For fourteen years she was no more than a scent and a nostalgia.

Her comeback set all the rules at nought. Exhausted with idleness, she started all over again. In 1953 Coco was seventy. Her three thousand employees were now only three hundred and fifty. It was the reign of Dior and his rigid style which dressed women in stiffened bodices and constricted waists. Chanel, with the same instinct as before, played the same trump: freedom of movement, suppleness, naturalness. She calmly set about producing 'Chanel' again. The first model appeared in a navy blue cardigan suit, labelled Numéro 5. Its simplicity took the journalists' breath away. Schiap, who on the mysterious departure of Mademoiselle Chanel thought she herself had descended on the world in a fiery parachute, declared: 'Chanel ees feeneesh!' In the silence of the return, *Le Figaro* wrote: 'It was touching. It was like being back in 1925.' Jaws worthy of Toulouse-Lautrec stretched forth to devour her. 'I prefer vitriol to honey,' said Chanel. 'The women will understand me.' *The Times* said, 'The buyers are buying.' *Life* photographed her models in the métro. Her little tweed suits with borders, the blouses to match the lining, and the chains, went round the world.

Her return was such a sensational success Chanel went to Dallas to receive the Neiman Marcus award for the most significant influence on the twentieth century. She wore her natural silk suit and raw silk blouse, her marvellous jewellery and the topaz an old lady who was fond of her gave her in Auvergne when she was sixteen: 'Take this, little Coco, and wear it always. It will bring you luck.'

'Luck is a mode of being, not just one little individual. Luck is my soul.' Chanel derived her elemental conquering force from her intimate contact with reality: it animated all her creations. 'Are there frills in the lines of an aircraft? No. I thought of aircraft when I created my collection.' She thought of what carries the fastest and the farthest.

The body was her limit, and she never went against it. She worked with her hands on the living model. Her staff followed her unflinchingly, passing the pins. 'My job is a bit above the factory,' said Coco, who would indefatigably take a suit to pieces as many as twenty-five times so that through it the woman who wore it could be seen and live. 'A suit only looks good when the woman who wears it seems to have nothing on underneath.' She was fiercely faithful to her alliance with the body. 'A sketch, a drawing – that's not the body. I don't sell bits of paper, and I don't charge for seats.' Chanel inhabited real life, and designed a real pocket in which a woman could keep her packet of cigarettes. 'A skirt should hug the legs, not float round them. That down to the knee, because women have to be seen. Below that, it's a question of the way you walk.' Chanel gave the lesson of her career to Hattie Carnegie, who said, 'She taught me everything.' But how? 'For example – never have a button without a button-hole.'

Mademoiselle. Keeping herself to herself. Up there in her rue Cambon, above the apartments, in the light of the roof

Coco in 1954, after her return to work

and the day. 'I'm listening to you,' she told me in the studio, 'but I'm also listening to my dress.' Madame Raymonde unrolled the fabrics. Chanel would tie knots in the samples, crumple them between finger and thumb, and hold them out in silence to her storekeeper. 'That's for bedspreads,' she'd say, a collar of faille samples round her neck over her navy blue suit. When a heavy white crêpe was spread out: 'For Liz Taylor on the Acropolis.' Chanel was chary of whites: 'It mustn't look like whipped cream.' Of Monsieur Bucol's tweed, 'It's too busy.' No one could rival Mademoiselle for recognising whether a tweed had really been made with the water of the Tweed. 'I only need to touch it.' She didn't stint herself. 'I don't make lamé blouses' – it isn't pleasant to the skin. Monsieur Bucol showed her a sequinned plastic. 'Sequins everywhere now, is it? It's a bit showy for me – more like the Galeries Lafayette. But find me some gossamer silk like this,' she said, putting her finger on the background of a spotted material.

Her flair was instinctive, as when she did the costumes for Cocteau's *Antigone*, dusting the actors with chalk and giving them white masks. They looked like statues, emerging from the night she reproduced from the blue of maids' overalls. Then over Antigone, stripped of everything, she threw her mantle, with crossed sleeves: that was Greece. 'Greece is wool, not silk. Men and women dressed in wool . . .' She refused to have anything to do with *La Machine infernale*: Jean had dressed his actors in towelling! 'Oh no, I'm not mixing myself up in that. But I'm quite willing to help you stick a few pins in at the last moment.' The theatre director asked: 'Cocteau, where are the characters supposed to enter?' 'He'd only forgotten to put doors in the set,' groaned Chanel. 'And what about the choruses?' demanded the director. 'You know, Jean,' she told him. 'Those things should be left to professionals.'

She never left anything to anyone else herself: she chose each piece of material personally. Her feeling for fabrics was

en 1937 – Robe du soir

Jean Cocteau
1937

The Incomparable Coco - Mademoiselle Chanel

'The incomparable Coco, Mademoiselle Chanel' by Cocteau

inimitable. She didn't have time for Italian tweeds: 'I saw
through them . . . And the more they're worked, the poorer
the quality gets.' The craftsman in her grumbled: 'What's the
point of bothering with tricks, when if the tension's right
any old merino is practically as good as cashmere? There
used to be a loom on the farms. Spinning's just a question of
tension.' Her ardent hand soon recognised what it rested on:
'I've seen plenty of cocoons. In Morocco they grow quite
fast. When the worm's in the cocoon it's stifled to death. I've
felt a skein of silk in my hand – you can sense that it's bene-
ficent.'

Chanel mistrusted colours not in nature, the colours of
bad taste: 'A pink that sets your teeth on edge! And when
you're right in the middle of your work and have to change
the thread every second . . .' What did she like? 'I take refuge
in beige because it's natural. Not dyed. Red, because it's the
colour of blood and we've so much inside us it's only right
to show a little outside.' Madame Raymonde kept a chart of
the chosen materials: the range of colours would have roused
Renoir's envy.

Then Mademoiselle went down into battle. A boxing-ring
never saw fiercer fighting. The spotlights converged mercilessly. Between the gilt panels of her sanctuary her model
advanced, took a few steps, then stood still before her. 'Come
nearer, child,' said Mademoiselle Chanel.

One needs to have watched her, neck hunched with the
fascination of a schoolgirl, ribboned hat on the brown curls,
standing stooped slightly forward – the unflagging movement
of her fingers, the shock of her passionate hand-to-hand
fight with metamorphosis. Catlike, Chanel stalked her prey
and never left it till it was conquered. 'Keep working till you
hate the sight of it.' Unerringly she undid seams, stripped off
mistakes fold by fold, girdled a dress round her like a rampart.
'All that's too small. I wish I ever got the chance to take
something away! The underarm is never big enough. And

once it's cut it's cut.' The cutters, nonplussed at the collapse of their models, watched as something very different from a dress was born: a love. Coco killed everything that conflicted with love, always on the alert to allow the body to blossom free of mannerism or disguise. She would prune and touch up and bare the shoulder so that it rose like a magnolia out of what had restrained it. 'Such stinginess, you can't move that sleeve – anyone would think the object was to be uncomfortable! You'd be dead after a day wearing this. These sleeves of yours look almost worn out already.' Her panelled skirts let the legs move forward freely. 'You should be able to see the thigh and everything that goes on, and it should be comfortable to wear. Cross your arms in front, child, you shouldn't ever move more than that. Put your hand in your pocket—it's deep enough, isn't it?' Chanel never strayed away from life; she concentrated on it with the rites of a conqueror. Her voice would grow husky, veiled with an authoritative mildness; she instructed, taught, in words patient or stubborn: 'It's too tight. Your blouse is here and now and it *is* the summer. A blouse shouldn't climb all over the place.' No detail was insignificant: 'What are these buttons? They're incredibly hideous – they look like poisoned chocolates.' Madame Raymonde would hurry over and hand her the tray with the intertwined C's. Her hand would hover over it with almost the gentle hesitation of the blind, then, finding its way, close round the rarely carved button she had made into a jewel.

Coco rebelled against a white hussar suit with striking, faultless braid: 'It's no good if a thing's only pretty as long as it's buttoned up. No woman will want to be imprisoned in that.' But many would have been if Chanel's most inflexible flair hadn't been for what is natural. She chastised, cut, and started again. 'How can you expect a sleeve like that to do on a modern dress? It's not difficult, Victor. It just has to follow the body of the wearer, not be all over the place. It's meant to fall straight over the shoulder-blades, not go bulging out like that! And you've even got the seat on the cross – it'll just bag, and the wearer won't be able to sit down in it.' She pricked her finger, under the nail. Her hands hurt. Arthritis lurked in the fingers covered with rings. But an invisible whip drove them on. 'As the peasants say, I've got chaps . . . At night I put surgical spirit on. It makes me howl, and I tell myself I'll shut up shop and abandon it all.'

All the time I knew her Chanel was preparing her 'last' collection. The rite had become an exorcism, but nothing ever made her swerve. Her fatalism, the experience of good luck and bad, her provincial sense of order, all made work an unfailing refuge for her. She was tanned with fatigue. 'Put two puckers here.' Her hands were spurred on now by excitement. The forewomen blinked, but followed her incorruptible course. 'You'll see how your sleeve will go now. The whole body has to feel dressed. Once you feel that, you know nothing can go wrong.' Trousers made her cross: 'It's been carried too far, degraded . . . I wear trousers in the country – you can fling yourself on the grass in them. In a dress you're worried in case it flies up. But these non-men! – that's different. They've made a religion out of being dirty. They don't wear stockings and they call that keeping cool. If I was a husband I'd say don't wear pants when you come out with me – I'm the one that wears the trousers.'

No one could take away her vision. 'Their eye and mine are two different things. Nothing in common. They like the street, they want to shock, they try to be amusing. For me, fashion's not amusing – it's something on the edge of suicide.' She caught hold of the edge of a skirt and criticised the unnecessary thickness. 'It's much prettier not to have a hem. Women don't need it – they're not going to grow any taller. It's the saleswomen – they arrange for clothes to be brought back and sold second-hand.'

Chanel had the hollow back of swift chargers. Proud and humble at once in the glare of the lights, she would never compromise. On the eve of the show she would undo the clothes yet again, raising the line of a grosgrain skirt over the little mountain-range of the hips. 'What's all this paraphernalia? Take it away, please, undo it. That's right, Manon – cry, go on, christen it.' After working hours on this model she saw it emerge garbled, mutilated. 'No, really, this is sabotage. I won't be put off like this, you shouldn't do it.' Irresistibly she begins again uncovering the lines of the body: 'They find the human body so repugnant they don't take it into account. I don't work for bread-boards. I can't bear people who're a-sexual.'

She radiated intolerance. 'They look at me dumbfounded and can't make it out. Everyone wants to keep on in the same old rut.' Then, in a murmur: 'These old queens . . . They stand on their dignity and put on airs of injured innocence like little girls. This one has his thumbs in the armholes of his waistcoat, that one is frivolous. Frivolity doesn't cut any ice.' She soon stirred them up: 'Jealousy is the most active of all muscles.'

The reduction by which she gave the body its destined freedom, despite the models' latent tendency to compromise, was the secret of a girl who had won out against the ladies. Her fine silhouette pitted itself against obstacles. She would stoop a little more, supple as seaweed driven by the sea. 'You have to find liberty. Liberate all those childish, ridiculous needs. The opposite of following the sketch. You haven't to skimp yourself, but really to give yourself room.' Ever since girlhood Coco had the instinct of command and a Manichaean sense of victor and vanquished.

'To discover a thing is to strip it to the quick,' said Braque. Chanel had discovered luxury and realised it ruthlessly. 'Simplicity doesn't mean poverty,' she'd say. Of an oriental tunic: 'That's not for doing the shopping in. Elegance means a thing's as beautiful on the wrong side as on the right.' She'd pinched the cuffs from the mandarins. An organdie dress followed: 'For a girl that's poor, with a body. And if you add a turban and a piece of jewellery, she can go into a restaurant and everyone will say, Isn't she pretty!' Then a suit of white

69

'Her fine silhouette pitted itself against obstacles.' Silhouette by Bérard

piqué appeared: 'I've cornered the market on piqué. And make a boater to go with it in the same material. When you've been drudging all day it's pleasant to put on something very clean. But you need to have a good laundress. The trouble is, it goes limp and flops all over the place. You can't control it.' A little blue silk suit reappears: '*You*'re an optimist! White buttons won't do – they look like eyes, like spectacles. And the twee, little-girl look . . .'

With anything over and above elegance, Chanel's hand was strict. 'Ah now, a white dress, I don't mind that at all, nice and fresh. Just right to go and say good morning to Monsieur de Gaulle. But take away a bit of the underskirt, eh? There, that's more human.' Elegance is sacrifice. Babbitt's America looked on in astonishment. Insipid roses disappeared from the stem of the torso: 'Take away all that jumble. I want a bunch of white grass.' A pink lamé was swathed in excited little flounces: 'Careful, it mustn't look Spanish!' Coco burst out laughing at exaggeration and ugliness. Her teeth sparkled savage and gay. The passionate mouth that scorned complaint acquiesced only in beauty.

She admonished a model: 'It's not supposed to be a race. I can understand you may find it boring, but in that case you should change your job.' Before how many stiff and sulky faces have I seen her reinvent grace and meaning. 'I need models who are beautiful,' she would murmur. 'And I've just got scrapings . . . There are some girls I simply can't work on, gargoyles.' They didn't last long: 'A touch of vulgarity finishes a dress for me.' She was famous for her Pygmalion-like power over the girls in white overalls girdled each with a tape-measure. They all wore Chanel sandals of beige kid, with toe-caps of black crêpe de Chine. 'When I think how I began by freeing women of this,' said Coco to me, pointing to her heel. She made the foot comfortable, rejecting shackles. 'I have my shoes too big – one day I just kicked one off. It's old-fashioned for a woman to show her feet just because they're small – it is abnormal, an anomaly.' Not a lock of hair escaped her decree:

'A poodle with a fancy trim sets the fashion nowadays. I like the girls to have their hair drawn straight back, and then any fullness brought forward to make the head look small. I don't know of a single fine portrait with lots of hair.' Alexandre's young friend came in with two curls behind the ear. 'I'm stalling him . . . He wants to catch me for a couple of thousand dollars' worth of hair. I shan't take any.' The models shrivel into dead leaves under make-up. Only the living hair shines above the jewels. There is nothing to torture or hamper: a gardenia is fixed to a comb so light you can't feel it, not so strong as a hairpin, yet it doesn't tremble in the chignon of the model who wears it, as she passes in a dark cloud of muslin, an elusive feminine mystery.

'They've killed luxury,' said Chanel. 'A woman goes out to dinner in dirty pants and a man's shirt. Squalor's the thing now.' She would never agree that fashion comes up from the streets. 'Fashions are good when they go down to them.' She wasn't bothered about being copied. She shook her head, laughing: 'I don't create fashion for three or four tarts.' But she had a passionate power of remaining aloof. She defended herself like a tigress against the all-invading mini-skirt, because knees aren't pretty. More fundamentally, she knew women lose everything if they renounce modesty. 'What's made for intimacy is exposed now. Exhibition is not my style at all. All this mutton dressed as lamb . . . the attempt to look young is enough to make them old.' Her secret was asking herself, as she looked at each model, whether she would wear it herself. 'If I say no, I leave it out of the collection. I have a horror of the ridiculous.'

Lewdness was lamentable. 'And it's all so dreary – people turn round just to see a couple of breasts, not very pretty and not clothed.' She never stopped denouncing sham. 'It's all this fancy dress that makes it difficult to work. Have you seen the latest *Vogue*? The women are barefoot. Lunacy. Back to the swamps. Soon we'll be having abstract women à la

Corbusier.' One gentleman was making dresses with nuts and bolts, another out of plastic. 'Fearsome,' shuddered Chanel, who couldn't bear a new suit: 'I put it on because I have to break it in. I feel as if I'm dressed in leather.' It wasn't long before dresses reached the pavement: 'The idiots get themselves up like priests now!'

When fashion is only a question of length, she declared, there will be no more fashion. She pulled her blue boater down further over her wilful fringe, and looked at you from beneath the little rampart. 'It comes from the peasants of La Mancha. I'd have liked to come from peasants. I always get on well with them.' Nothing ever made her give up her season. 'No one's presentable any more. I'm going to make dresses that are presentable. And they'll be women, not ragamuffins. Those who are unprepossessing . . .' She made a gesture of expulsion.

'Fashion's a flea-market now. They all vie to put forward the ugliest, the most garish. Everywhere "sales" and publicity – you can't turn round for them. And these "journaramas" – just filth. They add "rama" to everything this year. "Costurama" – what does that mean? It's just a fetish.' There was no nonchalance about her going into battle. 'Such trash leaves me with only one desire: to make things which are perfect,' she said, sitting down on her red chair.

She'd revived already, eager to cut down the forests of amateurs. So frail and tense, with her slenderness and sense of the absolute, she was like a suppliant about to burst forth into imprecations. 'Everyone's on their dignity here. That's no good to me – I've got a battle to fight. If you leave them to themselves,' she said of her staff, 'they'll stay with the same skirt twenty years. They're tense . . . They're afraid you might spoil a sleeve, and it's everything that needs to be destroyed!'

She snatched a band of bayadere from a waist. 'The tricks you have to have underneath for a dress to move well! That's fashion – what happens underneath. A summer dress is something constructed – otherwise, you can find a rag with a ribbon on it in any boutique. This is nothing, just off-the-peg stuff. I don't want to be disgraced.

'There are people,' she went on, 'who shut the shutters and don't want to see the light. A kind of inertia . . . You can kill yourself telling them how to work, you might as well talk to a brick wall.' Her look might be quizzing, severe, easy-going, curious or pleased: it always went with the same offertory gesture of the pins. They coursed over the girls' skins, harnessing, propping up, liberating. 'It makes a face here, your dress.' No botching up. She would take the whole thing to pieces again. 'My life doesn't depend on it, but yours does a bit,' she said, catching the foreman by his white overall.

Nothing was left to chance. Mademoiselle Chanel was as diligent as a bee to find the right place for a brooch. 'I can't bear it to wander about everywhere, and they might go and forget to put it on at all.' Between the thrills of ostrich feathers and illusions, her voice would be heard: 'Are the ear-rings clean?' The superfluities of a gold lamé were torn off: 'It ought to look like an improvised sweater. Make it as if it was wool, not gold. Remember, a woman is always too dressed and never sufficiently elegant.'

. Over-dressed: the English anathema was always before her eyes as she worked. 'We're going to wring the neck of magnificent gowns. It's better to be slightly under . . . If you're overdressed in your gown, you're the same with your umbrella, in the street, and in your mind. People like that get on my nerves!' When Jean was setting Marina off with necklaces, Chanel stopped him: 'No, no, she's a woman, not a shop window.' One magnificent necklace defined the neck, and she placed a chain very precisely to join a brooch she'd decreed should go on the side. 'You could put anything you like there now, even the order of the Holy Ghost.'

A spotted dress of navy and white twirled round. 'Pleats, Yvonne. It's an economical little dress. And tie a cravat under the collar.' The model Marina prevailed with icy passion.

'She's got Spanish bad taste – that's why I put up with her. French bad taste, now – that's the real thing.'

Neither agitation of nerves nor thunder-bolt of anger betrayed her. Her incantation would just become quieter: 'A bit loose, we need to sense the skin underneath.' A fresh young tailor-made of raw silk comes next: 'Now that's pretty. This little suit with nothing special about it, slim as slim, carry it to its logical conclusion.' Would she ever let up? 'Get me last season's jewellery. They haven't eaten it, I suppose?' She dismissed chains. 'Bazaar stuff, rue de Rivoli.' And to Madame Gripoix, holding out her latest-born: 'I'm against hugeness . . . Take a row away here and add a couple there.' Chanel moved buttons, replaced them, altered a balance, adjusted a collar. 'Put the collar in the middle, it shouldn't be lopsided. And that bead mustn't stick up, you'll have to put it lower down. Someone came yesterday to show me some jewellery. I told him you think we're still in the Middle Ages. You'd need to wear these on suits of armour, they're the size of saucepans. Jewels ought to look more real than the real thing. Craftsmen don't work seriously any more, they bet on horses.'

What she liked were the Florentine ornaments of the Medicis, and she thronged her dresses with Byzantine crosses. She would seize on them amorously among the trays of old pieces, recognise, reset them. 'When I have time I take a box of wax and make something with my hands. That's how I make my jewellery. Proportion is the thing.'

She liked saying: 'We're in trade, not art, and the soul of trade is good faith. Everything is alive, has a soul and an equilibrium. You can't create luxury out of trash.' All her senses were on the alert. 'When I can't make progress I can't see anything, just a white or grey flag.' Free of languor, she reacted to the physical poetry of her dresses, which travelled now in her stead: a suit of Gauguin blue, a tweed the colour of ripe corn, or a coat lined with wild llama, brought back the pinewoods to her, suntan, setting off. She started off again and disposed of the latest comer: 'They look at me bewildered and bring me the same old coat. I've worn a coat like that, with a little half-belt, ever since I was born! You should look something in a coat, not like a stick of bread but like those English portraits of women in riding habits.'

✳ 'You know you're a success, in fashion, if certain things are unbearable.' She would hold out through no matter what storms until she found what she wanted. 'You see, I said fur was difficult. Those are sleeves for athletes you've made there!' Linings of fawn, chestnut and black seal were lissom as kid gloves under the tweed. 'Fur is for inside, to keep you warm, stoke you up.' Then, indignant: 'Come now, I'm not going to have it calculated by the yard for a model. Tell him it's shabby. It reeks of the market stall a mile off – she looks as if she begged it off somebody. I've always told you we can't afford to buy cheap.' Black velvet opens on deep sable. Everything pretentious or obvious she secretly transfixed. Luxury is what is unseen.

She got out the astrakhan of her childhood and said, without batting an eyelid, 'Make hats of it.' Wouldn't she trip on the carpet covered with pins? Around her, shoulders sag, dark rings deepen under eyes, tape-measures bulge round the white overalls, the forewomen sit near the little red chair with its spools of coloured tape and box of sweets. She goes on, still standing. One of her swift smiles transfigures her face: 'Prestige is my business. In all the nominations of ministers and presidents, I've never once heard the word prestige.'

Her curious, obstinate, animal pride served her uncompromisingly. 'I suffer like a dog because I hate mediocrity.' She would not flag till the collection was over. 'If I start getting stuck to my chair . . .' She was tired out. Madame Raymonde offered the little suède cushion. 'No, no cushion – it makes me sink back and then I can't get up again. You can't abandon a collection unless it abandons you. I don't believe in bowing the neck. I've got the most awful stage-fright.'

Her fight was also with her staff. They shared the toll of

'She got out the astrakhan of her childhood and said, "Make hats of it."'

One of the dinners for the staff given before every collection. Coco at the back, with Paul Iribe

weariness. 'From me they accept anything. But in front of strangers they don't like to stand up for themselves. I see all that and I won't let anyone come. Work doesn't need an audience. Yesterday someone was coming up and I rushed and said: "No, don't hurry, it's not worth it, you're only going to have to go down again. I'm too much on edge."' I was allowed a chair behind her. 'Keep quiet. Bad work gets what it deserves. I'm not going to put out bad work. Certainly not!' She showed me her nails, all the varnish chipped off: 'I make use of my nails – it's them I hang on with.' Her intransigence had no equal: 'I keep it up until they do what I want . . . Them and their optimism! Always sure everything is all right.'

Fashion was being choked to death by amateurs, she would tell anyone who'd listen. 'All these amateurs . . . I think it's time the professionals withdrew. If I close down I'll make sure it causes as big a row as possible while I'm about it.' But the abdication didn't come. 'The answer isn't to climb down but to rise higher. If I just avoided giving offence, if my collections just repeated themselves, I'd produce trash.' She was tired now and worked sitting down, indefatigably, getting up to see to an armhole. 'Make the sleeve a bit bigger, it looks like a stove-pipe.' Her voice was almost inaudible. 'If I shut my eyes I fall asleep. But I'm a craftsman – I work as if I had to earn a living.'

The rays of her perfume grew fainter. Outside, night lowered, shadow deepened. The petals of day were scattered beneath its black pistil. I've seen her make childlike attempts – the unforgettable halts on the stairs, sudden spurts of conversation, other marvels of dissimulation – which only tried to deceive her own poignant fear of finding herself alone, abandoned. But the ambush in which she held whoever she retained would eventually leave her with the poisoned dart of her solitude. She never acquiesced in it.

It was Friday. 'This evening they'll say, "Have a good weekend, Mademoiselle." Then there'll be the usual rush to fly about amusing themselves. They celebrate defeats if there aren't enough victories. The three-day week. They won't remember anything by Monday. When I look at the suburbs . . .'

That Saturday before the 14th of July, when everyone was there against their will, models, forewomen, cutters, workroom staff, she had to animate this inert and hostile tide. Coco didn't care a hang: she would go right through with it, she'd undo everything. Six o'clock came. Madame Raymonde took off the long white bond of her scissors. 'What, finished?' Coco had taken off her cravat and put a little scarf round her neck. A red scarf. Everyone ground their teeth, but this didn't lessen her wrath an atom. 'They don't want to work. They're like the students.' Her remedy for the latter was breaking stones on the roads. 'In the old days it said in the books that work ennobled man. Now it disgraces him.' The place emptied. A girl went by with loads of fur over her arm. All that was left were threads on the floor.

Her ardent monologue didn't flag. 'It's the farmer in me that works. The word vacation brings me out in a sweat. When they come back they don't know where they are. They need another holiday before they can start work again.' But the geysers of her wrath soon make them feel at home: 'All pals together – I should say so! I'm not going to let myself be trampled on in the very firm I created. Let myself get maty with everyone – perish the thought! Every man to his trade. People want you to be gentle. Gentleness doesn't get work done, it isn't true. Unless you happen to be a hen laying eggs. It's anger that gets work done.' Her words, her effervescence, leaped like bubbles against the wall of solitude.

'But there's plenty of time, Mademoiselle.'

⸙ 'It's always later than you think.'

She drew from among the black-numbered, white plastic cards: this was the supreme lottery, and Madame Raymonde noted in blue pencil the lucky numbers. 'It's like baccarat,' said Chanel, fingering her necklace of stones from the Urals. Any of the models might fall victim to her exorcism: 'Maïa is in a bad temper. I've never been able to stand a model who sulks. I won't sacrifice a dress! Maïa's out of date, she looks like a lady, and no one wants to look like that now.' She transferred all her dresses to the radiant Betsy. 'The other one crushed all the life out of them.'

Coco sculpted each dress for a woman who might meet her fate wearing it. Insolent, accurate, she trusted to her instinct alone. With her scissors and seeing hands, she gave our angst-ridden age a chance to breathe. 'I still have ardour left,' she used to say to me. 'It's the only force that doesn't grow humble with time.'

Fatigue and admiration made the silence iridescent. The building emptied as the hundreds of little hands left. Boxes of flowers and ribbons disappeared behind screens. Madame Raymonde unhooked the scissors from round Mademoiselle's neck. It was the final rite before all that space became superfluous once more. The dresses were taken away, white ghosts tied up in sheets. The cutters and forewomen came down in their street clothes, human beings again like everyone else, the great transfiguration of the work left behind.

As the spell of work lost its power, Chanel went up between the mirrors, elegant as an antelope, back to her glade.

The bunch of spectators took the red seats by storm. At the top of her magic stairs assailed by mirrors, a slender shape, hatted, sat on a step and gazed intently. Apprentices, awkward in their flowered overalls, religious medals hanging round their necks beside needlecases of black leather, brought down the last dresses from the workrooms. American journalists pointed out the celebrities to one another: from the wife of the Prime Minister to actresses, all come in search of manna from the most imitated woman in the world. Annie Girardot lit a Gitane beside Luchino Visconti. A shrubbery of murmurs spread, stopped, and was suddenly scythed by silence: the show had begun.

'A collection is like a play: I hear the deathly silence in which a coat will pass, and have to take my cue.' She sensed her audience instantaneously. A rhapsodical certainty was switched on like a current. 'When they're successful from top to bottom you can tell as soon as they enter,' she said of her clothes. 'It isn't amateurism – I'd never have gone in for that.' The applause was evidence enough. But her triumph didn't weaken her rule: it only made it stronger, like the slender body bent daily to the task. She found all these compliments rather contemptible: 'I'm not entirely satisfied,' she told her admirers. What she wanted to create was illusion.

'I'm fed up with hearing about "the little Chanel suit." '

Marlene Dietrich kissed her hand in the German fashion. The band of the faithful was no more than a crowd of shades disappearing into the night. After reprimanding her models, seeing her forewomen, and announcing that work would start again next day, Chanel, who'd gone to bed at three that morning, only said in that voice full of passion: 'I'm bored to extinction!'

The Everyday

What accustomed me to such a modest use
of my leisure, so daily a return to what awaits
me? I think it was the provinces, and their
naïve belief that regularity has some votive
power . . . It isn't that my own plot appeals
to me every day. COLETTE

The Everyday

A lady asked Chanel, 'What do you have for breakfast?' 'A camellia, Madame, and for dinner an orchid.'

'I don't live in the ether,' laughed Chanel. Her spontaneity was ballasted with life.

'It's the everyday that's so hard to put up with. In literature the everyday doesn't exist.' The only struggle that interested her was the one with her own Sisyphean boulder – as Reverdy said, 'the only adventure, the one that lasts, in other words life, sealed up, inexpressible, even the simplest, that ardent life of the prisoner with both eyes avidly fixed on the peep-hole.'

Coco battled with dresses, but the single combat never wore her out. A silk muslin scarf round her neck fastened with a jewelled clip, her felt or straw boater perched smartly on her fringe, with long supple boots under a cardigan and skirt, she never left home, all the days God sent, without scenting her clothes. Her handkerchief, a perfumed wad, was in her pocket – white, provincial, cotton, everyday. She changed it as one changes one's linen. Up in her store-room Madame Raymonde could tell by sniffing whether Mademoiselle had arrived.

She left a wake of perfume. 'They say I smell nice: of course I do, I know how to use scent! The French put a dab behind each ear, and one little bottle lasts them six months. And they call that using perfume.' When the manager of a scent factory went away he could easily tell which of his samples Mademoiselle's nose had selected: 'The bottle where there's hardly any left. I have my own way of using scent.' She wanted to find a perfume for men: 'It mustn't be oriental. Musk and incense are feminine.' She battled with phials as she did with the pilasters of material. 'A perfume should be sweet, but they do everything to make it lose its sweetness.' She didn't like gardenia: 'Too sugary.' But intensity was important too: 'A perfume *ought* to smell too strong. And they bring you tepid water.' Her sense of smell was fierce: 'In the lily of the valley they sell on the 1st of May, I can smell the hands of the kid who picked it.' Of the boxes of Number 19 opposite, she told Maître Chaillet, her lawyer: 'A perfume ought to punch you right on the nose. You don't expect me to sniff for three days, do you, to see if it smells or not? It has to have body, and what gives a perfume body is the most expensive thing there is.'

Her perfume paid her back. It made her one of the richest women in the world. But, as Colette perceived, she gave off no trace of 'the contagious dazzle of gold.' For Coco money had only one meaning: freedom. 'Money is pocket-money.' From her strawberry grosgrain purse she would draw out new and neatly folded notes: 'I'm always very respectful with money. Tips are money invested for comfort. They feel a bit of affection for you instead of spitting in your eye.' The rest slumbered in Switzerland. 'Money's not becoming to women. It makes them think they can do anything they like.' She hated the millstone and the cult of wealth: 'Some people grow poor by saving and others get rich by spending. I've always been as poor as Croesus and as rich as Job.'

Every day at one she would go up the stairs in the rue Cambon to her apartment, like Napoleon. Her guards were the mirrors, straight to attention from the mezzanine to the second floor. There would be a few halts on the way, her gaze plumbing yours – perhaps a ruse to prevent the stairs knowing they'd made her short of breath. Two young messenger-boys rushed down the stairs without any greeting. 'What manners. All Monsieur Freud's fault! According to him it's all an illness.'

Once over the threshold we were in China. 'When I've unfolded my screens in my little retreat . . .' On the Coromandel table, a compass. When she'd taken her watch with the white leather strap off her wrist to give to Hélène Lazareff, she got a new one from Switzerland. 'Mademoiselle, you can't have a chromium watch!' 'Of course I can. A watch is like a saucepan in a kitchen. It's for telling the time. If I was in a kitchen I'd put a saucepan there,' she said, looking at the watch-face from Lausanne, that she was going to have mounted so that it would stand flat on her Chinese table. 'Not one of those little microbes from Cartier's.' Pascal emerged in a white jacket from the folds of dark lacquer which hid the doors: 'Mademoiselle, lunch is served.'

'I've always lived in either attics or palaces. I don't want any more palaces, but I do like to keep a good table.' Candour sparkled between her little white China monkey, which she stroked, and the prongs of her fork. Unexpected guests arrived: they were her souvenirs.

'Cocteau was well bred. He never spoke about himself, he was a bourgeois. He had no talent, so he listened . . . Just a little tiny bourgeois who tried to steal novelty.' The nomad couldn't bear the family Muse: she imitated Cocteau's *Maman!* without any concession to the silver cord. 'If you'd seen old Mother Cocteau! Mean! An ancient out of tune piano, and they invited Marcelle Meyer to come and sing. It was as if someone invited me to a dinner-party and then asked me to run up a dress! She was appalled at the thought of how much the disintoxication cure was going to cost.' In Jean's room, Coco recalled, there wasn't one picture: just a piece of paper with a dice, by Picasso. But he was amusing. During Guitry's play, when Guitry's wife was just poised to resume her career as a dancer, Cocteau ripped up a piece of calico at exactly the right moment. The audience burst out laughing.

She very much liked the speech of the member who welcomed Cocteau into the Academy, and recognised his familiar, 'It's you who were the poem.' But what he didn't say, she went on, was that he was a bourgeois and a milksop.

'He took to his bed when Radiguet died, and gave out that he was ill. He was no more ill than you or I.'

Radiguet for her was 'the Cocteau impedimenta,' the night-club *Le Boeuf sur le Toit*. 'There was a fellow there called Moyzès' – she pronounced it Moses – 'who came to me and said, "Monsieur Cocteau never pays." I paid for three weeks, but after that I said no, nothing doing!' The blunders of adolescence didn't interest her. Radiguet? 'A dud. That's why he died so young. He hated Cocteau. One day at my place Jean started to talk about society people. Oh, said Radiguet, you're better at that performance than anyone.' A reporter asked earnestly what Radiguet would have become if he'd lived. 'A little man of letters,' came the answer.

'Cocteau decked himself with young men like a woman who hangs orchids round her face and destroys them. In America they used to send me orchids before dinner and I used to say put them in the ice-box. Imagine wearing something that dies on you – if I wear a flower it's an artificial one.'

Coco served life without concession. 'I've always said yes to life.' And she recalled Al Brown, the former boxing champion, who took to drugs with Bébé Bérard and Cocteau. He had an oblong dancer's body which she disliked, with hands that were too long, and Cocteau had him sent to the mental hospital at Charenton. When he came out he came to her, penniless. In New York she noticed the porter's voice drop announcing his arrival. She told Brown the truth. 'You're a fallen champion. No one wants to see you any more. Win again, and you'll have everyone at your feet.' She arranged for him to train at Chantilly, telling the trainer: 'If it goes well I'll pay. If it doesn't, tell me, and I'll stop.'

She wouldn't go with Cocteau to Brown's comeback: 'No, you're too conspicuous.' But she dined in a Russian night-club and found herself sitting two rows behind Cocteau and Bérard at the match. They didn't see her. Al Brown saw her at once, and winked: 'Blacks are so intelligent.' There were to be five rounds. A man sitting beside her in the dark said

Brown wouldn't be able to take it. 'Champagne ruins a boxer's stomach.' Coco at once riposted that he'd be all right, he'd been in training. 'What do you know about it?' Every time Brown was knocked down her neighbour dug her in the ribs, and when the lights went up she saw by his broken nose and the rest that he was a boxer.

In the third round Brown's wink was a long one and he delivered a knock-out. He appeared in his dressing-gown, declining to be massaged, and the crowd was milling round to congratulate him. A policeman barred Coco's way, saying: 'No women allowed in.' She felt like crying and disappearing, and sent a message in by her escort, Félix Rollo.

She was afraid of crowds. 'Once when Cocteau had taken Georges Auric and me to the Théâtre Saint-Martin, Auric was making fun of the hypnotist, who sensed there was an enemy present. He wasn't interested in me – I'd have resisted. He asked fat Auric to go up on the stage: I can still see him getting up, large and dignified, going up, shaking hands, lying down, and coming back to his seat without realising what had been happening. He looked like a shattered old woman. All I wanted to do was get away. I nudged Cocteau and said: "Get me out of here!" Everyone was looking at us. I didn't breathe until I was back in the car. "Home right away," I told the mechanic.'

In her youth she used to faint. When her Englishmen took her on the roller-coaster in Luna Park they made her put her head on their shoulder: 'Don't be frightened, we're here.' 'You talk to me as if I were a pet dog,' she said, and yelled as loud as she could. 'It was because of that I stopped going to mass. I used to tell myself I was going to faint, and the mere thought is enough to make it happen.'

Her frankness was legendary. One day Gala Dali objected to what people said about Picasso, and Coco answered: 'My dear, he's neither the idiot you say, nor the genius everyone else claims.' 'And where would you place Dali?' asked Gala. They'd been eating green peas, and there was one left on

'Little Dali, little Gala. They used to squat like a couple of birds.'
Dali and Gala at La Pausa

Coco's plate. She gave it a flick with her finger: 'There.'

'Little Dali, little Gala. They used to squat like a couple of
birds and swap smutty stories, moustache in air.' When Coco
first met him Dali was handsome. 'He wore a carnation behind
his ear to take the smell away – he used to eat tins of sardines
and put the oil on his hair.' Her strangest reminiscence of
America was of Dali taking her to one of the most daring

spots in Harlem, watched by the the police. There were black musicians making love with their instruments. They began with a very soft tune which worked up to a frenzy: 'A cry of love, you see.' The player and his saxophone were one. And, dancing, the woman drew back and drew back, but all the time she was languorous, inviting, echoing the sinuous movements of the man. 'It was the simulacrum of love, as the mass is the simulacrum of God: the dances they sweat over now are nothing at all. That was sacred. To try to imitate it is like breaking a cross to pieces and prancing about with them.'

Dali and Gala drank it up with all their eyes, but when Dali asked her what she thought: 'I said, "It's sublime. But it's not sublime for us to be here. Let's go." '

By nature she was an eternal schoolgirl, always eager to learn, to watch, to recognise. And to denounce as well. Her conversation was a guillotine that fell mercilessly on every kind of wig: she hated sham, whether that of society, money, or the false assumption of talent.

She sighed over the socialites. 'What people call society, and what they won't do to be part of it! As far as I can see, it's always a bit "high"; you'd need to pickle it to make it keep. The divine body stinks.' Then a barricade over her face. 'I wasn't "well-born." I don't give a damn for the Almanach de Gotha.' She shunned parties where the talk was gossip and the so-called pleasure 'unbelievable chaos.' An enjoyable party was one where people were flayed alive. 'You see them devouring each other. Someone should introduce a language for society in which scandal isn't admissible.' She delighted in one woman's comment on what people said about her behind her back: 'My arse is deaf.'

She told me the English put the old Aga Khan behind a screen so as not to see him. 'I took the screen away and asked him to lunch.' She saw him again in Geneva; she was fascinated by the tang he had, his clan, his mystery. 'A different sort of thing from the Prince of Monaco, after all: he rules over millions of souls, not a few croupiers.' 'I'm very fond of my Ismailis,' he told her. 'To think that all I know of France is the spas. I go there to make myself ashamed of myself and to see people who are the opposite of me.' 'Be very tough with the English,' she advised him. 'Thank you. You give me heart.'

Coco had her own definition of snobbishness: 'Being too polite to people who are not polite enough to you.' She was never impressed by money. When Maurice de Rothschild showed her his showcases she said: 'Yes, very pretty. I wouldn't mind wearing one of those jewelled shells on my head or round my neck.' He said: 'But do you know what that is?' 'Of course – Renaissance, Benvenuto Cellini.' He was terrified and pulled her away: 'Let's go and have coffee.' 'I wanted to take him down a peg or two.'

She never forgot the warning Madame de Chévigné gave her when she was twenty: 'My child, all men are pimps.' The last of the knights, she'd sigh. She was too lucid to be taken in: 'One's surrounded by this wonderful public, but it's only money that really gets them moving. As soon as money's mentioned they're all over you. What with those who'd do anything for money and those who'd do anything for art, I think I'm going barmy.'

Vulgarity and bad taste were her bane. She said of a lady who chose a poor specimen of a lover: 'If you're dying of hunger you'll eat a rat.' At a performance of Feydeau's *A Flea in her Ear*, the audience laughed at the word 'cuckold'. 'How are you to make an audience of illiterates laugh? It's degrading. If I'd had a whistle I'd have whistled. But I hadn't.' The front rows of the stalls were covered in flowers. 'I asked if that's where the corpse was – it looked like a funeral. Not at all. It was for the important people, to separate them from common mortals.'

She used to say to me: 'When I landed back in France I didn't know the French.' She never forgave them for not having been part of her romantic youth. 'Eyes like chickens . . .

Their little house, their little garden, their little village – they use the word "little" in front of everything.' One day she arrived at a dinner-party and announced: 'Mosquito has won the golden guitar.' Everyone burst out laughing. The pop singers held their jamborees at the Olympia music-hall at the end of the rue Cambon. 'They won't last – that's why they fling themselves about.' Such buffoonery left her cold. ' "Keep my sweat, it will bring you luck." They're right next-door to Our Lady of Lisieux.' Of Monsieur Johnny Halliday: 'Shaking himself about like that, he's bound to collapse in the end. And we're supposed to swallow his nightmares. Well, I'm not likely to wear out the seats.' He writhed about in sequins, bare-chested, and only found favour with her when he fought and got a bloody nose with a professional boxer in the audience. 'But he throws himself about, he works . . . If I could do it I would, every morning,' she said, looking in the glass. The panther pants from the earthly paradise didn't impress her. 'He just wants to sweat. Then he flings off his smelly clothes, one by one. The fans catch them, but he isn't giving anything away: they pay him back. Those people wouldn't give away a handkerchief.'

The antique chocolate-pot appeared, with the arms of Scotland on it and a rose on the lid. When I asked where we should have coffee, she said: 'Here – if we go into the next room it'll take us ten minutes to settle down.' Then, pointing to the cool wooden handle on the hot enamel: 'You see, it's for use, not for ornament.' Her television set was opposite, on its pragmatic pedestal. 'It's like the plate you eat off. And some people try to hide it!' The small ember of her cigarette sparkled under the boater still resting on her curls. 'It's so that my hair stays done all day. And also, I admit, a habit I adopted in self-defence. When someone boring came I could always say I was just going out.'

Her art of living was a mixture of the sturdy stock of the provinces, the astringent elegance of Ascot, and the dream of Bohemia. She adored trains. 'You can get all the masterpieces in paperback at the stations.' On the Transalpin, which took her to Switzerland, and on which the waiters were Italian, she used to go to the restaurant car when everyone else had finished, and order eggs or ham. 'I'd rather do that than stay in my compartment where they're all asleep with their mouths open. I give the waiters three francs instead of one. I can't bear people who travel glued to their wallet, and always on their dignity. Maggie de Zuylen used to ask if the service was included when they brought the bill. I said, No, one always leaves something for the enjoyment. Large or small . . .'

I can see her at nine-thirty – she used to get up late – all ready at the Ritz, putting away pots of cream and little plastic holders on her dressing-table, throwing away a box of rice-powder. 'That Germaine,' she said, of her old lady's-maid from the Landes, 'she's a hoarder. It gets so a cat couldn't find her kittens.' Germaine passed through. She picked up a rusk, wrapped it in a paper tissue, and put it away in a drawer. 'She's a peasant. She can't bring herself to throw medicine away. I used to have to take her everywhere with her sister or she would have died of jealousy.' Jeanne, her finer sister, was dead. 'But,' sighed Coco, 'I'm not going to jump out of the frying pan into the fire! I wash everything myself – my comb, my stockings.' Over her turban she wore a marvellous bow loosely tied under her chin, which would have made her look like a colonial soldier only that it was of silk. Germaine appeared again with a little felt hat on her head: 'So, Germanicus – you're imitating me. Look,' she said to me: on Germaine's artificial astrakhan collar there were a couple of grey hairs.

The little lift attendant held the impatient elevator. She drew a note, new and folded, from her long shoulder-bag. 'But you gave me something yesterday, Mademoiselle.' 'It's your lucky day then.' And turning to me she confided: 'They change every day. There was a little bell-hop who made eyes. He didn't last long!' She called her handbag her cemetery. 'The thought of moving all these dead bodies . . .' The flashing zip shut on the wallet full of new notes and on sheaves of pending correspondence. A slim, youthful silhouette in a tweed suit disappeared into the back of the sleek black Cadillac driving off to Switzerland.

'When I fly I always hold on to the seat-belt – I never fasten it. Too frightened I couldn't get out if the plane caught fire.' Nor could she do with Sunday drivers. 'Imagine finding myself with a policeman breathing into my face!' She was enchanted by the silos and the state highways. 'We go at such a lick – like a switchback! We make Vadim look older than Monsieur de Pourtalès.' Monsieur de Pourtalès, a grey old gentleman, spent several months in the salon in the rue Cambon. Going down a specially precipitous slope she would sing *Tosca* and *Manon*. 'We might try *Parsifal*! It's because I've always sung as I drive that I've got so little voice left.' And she would start to hum a song about spring:

> '*Beginning of spring*
> *Singing of hope*
> *The world is late*
> *The earth is young.*'

She loved the smell of the forest; snow reminded her of Saint-Moritz where she met Emilio Pucci, always falling over but always well dressed. 'Stick to haute couture,' she told him. Seeing a boy of twelve ski-ing away merrily, she took off alone on the slopes. Her instructor did her boots up so tight they hurt; he always insisted on doing it himself, and on hanging her socks up to dry. 'He was like a chambermaid. Then he told me, "When you fall down, just sit – I'll come and pick you up." ' He went off and left her, and she stopped falling over. She'd ski all morning and wait in the tearoom for the sledge to take her back to the hotel. 'And they'd send me the bill – just for 50 yards. Do they take me for a fool just because I don't know how to put on airs and light my own cigarette? The sparks burn my fingers, and if I'm in bed I set fire to the sheets. I could never do that – I've always had a man or men

Coco at Saint-Moritz

to do it for me.' She broke her ankle, started ski-ing again,
but at that point decided she'd had enough of sport. 'I loathe
obligations. I've never given in to them. The obligation to
ski is the same as all the rest. And the idea of going back every
year . . . what a bore.'

' "I was passing by the Tuileries . . . It's the season for
love." ' Yvonne Printemps, unforgotten. ' "And be sure to
write and tell me you miss me terribly." Reynaldo Hahn
used to say she got on his nerves. He played the piano char-
mingly, only he was dull as ditchwater and full of complexes.
The one I *don't* like is Auric. I left him and his wife in my
house at Roquebrune and one day when they were drinking
and playing about he upset a bottle of champagne over the

piano. An artist doesn't do that. I wouldn't do it to a mouth-organ.'

We'd stopped in a bistrot. 'We're unaccompanied, but who cares. Order.' No first course, just escalope and steak with endives and spaghetti. It was awful. Very sweetly she said it was very nice, and we still had the bottle of Beaujolais. 'I asked for the dearest, at five francs. And for some blue cheese. One ought to be able to pig it sometimes, know how to take one's high hat off.' She recited La Fontaine's fables, the grass-hopper and the ant, the wolf and the lamb, the ploughman and his children. She knew La Fontaine by heart, and was she so very far away from him? 'You can't improve people with money. Money is a good servant and a bad master.'

'Germaine, what did you have?' 'I'd have liked coq au vin – I had that once with Madame la baronne's Joseph, and it brought back memories. I had some fillets of perch and some soup. But you were up at a quarter past seven this morning, Mademoiselle, and you have to get up early to-morrow to see the house.' Coco was looking for a house in Switzerland. 'If it's no good we'll visit orphanages and have porridge.' Germaine took her up: 'You haven't anything to do in the afternoon, Mademoiselle.' 'What do you mean, nothing to do? Are you my governess? Are you going to give me orders? What are you going to do?' Germaine laughed: 'Wash and iron Mademoiselle's things.' 'There won't be much to-morrow – a slip and a brassière for my enormous bosom.' She told me Germaine loved her like a dog and she kept her for her laugh. Coco called Germaine her mentor.

Canals. 'The Burgundy, the Rhine canal . . . I wanted to visit all the canals with someone I loved, all the way to Con-stantinople. The houses by the locks – they're all alike. Where the yacht or the barge has to go through.'

As soon as we got to the Lausanne Palace Hotel her books were scattered over the bed, among them the Confessions of St Augustine. 'So many things in it that are touching, familiar. It all goes on inside me, in the huge palace of my memory.'

She tied her kerchief over her head and fingered her pearls. 'I'm a gipsy, you know. When you travel you should forget everything else, otherwise you travel like a grande dame and are bored to death.'

I've seen her relax like an animal, in white silk pyjamas, her scarf tied over her curls, the Swiss gipsy, forgetting all about time. 'I hate habits.' She would sleep with bare feet, like an Arab. If she felt cold she would drape a towel over herself, and the icy air would be filled with some tropical languor. On her bedside table the three faces of the icon Stravinsky gave her kept the Slav secrets of a psalm. She would never be parted from her talismans. As for all the rest, she'd leave it behind without a thought. A gull struck the window with its beak. 'I hate those birds.' She couldn't bear the dampness of the lake, the sewerage of Switzerland. What fluttered in the air for her were her places, her feelings, the gipsy in her.

'The new-mown hay and the tall steeples,' she said, showing the Russian chalets on the fly-leaf of her book. She didn't like the revival of *The Idiot*. 'They shout . . . If you'd seen Madame Pitoëff – just the opposite! The merchant goes mad. That's Russian drama – someone drops a handkerchief without raising his voice, and it's all the tragedy in the world. It's not restrained. Art is made out of imperfection.' Russian tears, oblivion and pain tremble on the garden knife.

Italy came back to her, and her capers there, and the white beans of Florence cooked in oil. 'The only thing you can eat. The Italians put cheese on everything.' She liked the churches in Modena. 'Skeletons. Just frames of wood. On the way to Venice she stopped in Milan where the Visconti boys waited for her at the station.' ' "No, I'm not free for lunch" . . . I was dining with their father in the old palace. He told me he wanted to talk to me about Luchino. "Do you like oil-cloth, Mademoiselle?" he asked me. "Luchino's surrounded by it. All his curtains are made of it, and he's arranged rows of Eiffel Towers on the mantelpiece." ' Coco told him she abominated oil-cloth and couldn't bear the smell. 'My sister

Luchino Visconti

and I hated everything familiar to us, including tables covered with oil-cloth. We felt people weren't going to much trouble for us.' Visconti complained that his sons found his glass-fronted cabinets old-fashioned and had made him have them removed. A grand seigneur, he passed over morality: 'Every man to his taste.'

'I don't like Italians,' she told me. 'They're women dressed up as men.' But America attracted her, America, which had taken her father away and whose daughter she was by adoption. 'Chanel is as American as hamburger.' Westerns and the wide open spaces captivated her. In 1929, at the invitation of Sam Goldwyn, she made her famous trip to New York. 'The

Americans wanted to tie me down, you see, because I out-fashion fashion. But I'm not for sale or hire. In Hollywood the stars are just the producers' servants.' Coco would never be ruled by anyone else. 'Jean Harlow was always waggling her ass, looking for millionaires.' Garbo used to tell her: 'I wouldn't have existed, in my hat and raincoat, if it hadn't been for you.' Coco remembered her big feet, the way she used to kick her shoes off so as to be more natural, and her humility. 'Garbo had realised important dresses didn't suit her, that she needed to be humble . . .'

The man she called 'Mother' went with her and though he was a Jew himself wouldn't allow his co-religionists near. Coco was impatient: she'd just met Maurice Sachs again. 'I prefer my Jewish friends to lots of Christians, the St Cretin variety,' she used to say. 'There are the great Jews, the Hebrews in general, and the Yids. But all we've got are tramps.' She loved her Jewish doctor better than all her family. The son of a seller of suits and braces whose seven sons all

Misia Sert

became doctors, he was a friend of Sarah Bernhardt's father. The actress's father had the same strange eyes as his daughter and used to sell razors. He would arrive at farms when the men were in the fields, glare round, and empty out his wares. 'Who wants to buy a razor?' The women were so terrified they bought the lot.

On a roof in San Francisco, after a Chinese theatre performance during which Misia Sert had gone to sleep, Chanel heard a black singing 'My Woman':

> *My woman is mean as she can be*
> *my woman she makes a fool of me*
> *never treats me good*
> *I don't care*
> *for I love her*
> *she is lying when she says I love you*
> *I know it but what am I going to do*
> *never treats me good*
> *I don't care for I love her*
> *once I laughed at love*
> *it is all wrong*
> *then you came along*
> *with a new song.*
> *Now I sing a blue song*
> *my woman she has a heart of stone*
> *not human but she is my own*
> *till the day I die*
> *I'll be loving my woman.*

At Beverley Hills she and Misia searched for the name of the Mdivani brothers beyond the beaches, among the oil-wells. 'He's married a company, not a girl.' They passed gate-post after gate-post. 'Misia was deaf – that is, she didn't understand English. Mdivani had told me, go along the beach and you get to my house. But on the posts, instead of Mdivani, there was written Chanel. Misia said: "It's your father. We'll find him and take him back with us. I'll leave Sert."' Coco, who always called a spade a spade, retorted that she'd done that already. Misia, with her Polish jealousy and love of tragedy, had a great affection for Roussy, with her halo of defeat, with whom Sert had fallen in love. 'Roussy was a backward little girl whose only bad taste was to fall in love with Sert . . . Her father and brothers were marvellously good-looking. So for her a handsome man was someone as different as possible from them – like Sert, an old boy with a beard. She thought he was gifted.' Coco had told Sert outright what she thought of his painting, in her version of Spanish, in the Café de Paris: *merda horrora*. Sert had overturned the table, then knelt on the pavement to beg her to come back. 'I gave Misia a mother-of-pearl bedroom suite,' she said. 'Misia sold it to Elizabeth Arden. Mother-of-pearl! Can't stand it. I had pearl.'

She described the four television sets that were waiting for her in Hollywood on a later trip: two bedrooms, a sitting-room, and a bathroom where she could see the screen from the bath. 'All that's for people who've gone soft. The English hide everything, the Americans show everything! America is dying of comfort. That's why they'll buy every luxury, and the first of all luxuries is perfume. Hotels. Luxury will end up not being French any more! But there's one thing that's not for sale, and that's Mademoiselle Chanel.'

Coco never had and never would read *Alice in Wonderland*, but she liked *A Pilgrim Shadow in Search of Eldorado* and hated Disney. How could she like the magician of childhood? An ice-hockey match in Toronto, the great leg-guards, enchanted her: 'The pads were red, enormous. The place was full of blacks and the air was blue with the glow of cigarettes.' She wore white boots trimmed with black that she'd bought in New York, and her llama coat. 'People said, "You can't beat Paris!" And it all came from America!'

People are made up of habits, she said. When you're used to a seventh floor with a balcony you can't live on a mezzanine any more. 'When I got to know the Waldorf Astoria I always took rooms high up. But I used to say to the porter, "Come into the street." "The street? But it's stifling in the street!" "Maybe, but in here I'm freezing." ' One evening she went out to dinner, and her hostess opened the door with her dress tucked up and wearing a white apron. 'The cook. And kitchens terrify me, I told her. The butter spurts all over you and your clothes are ruined for the evening.' 'Yes,' said her hostess, 'but come with me to the kitchen, because all the flowers are in the Frigidaire.'

When she went back to America she was greeted with escorts of cars, which she hated and thought crazy. 'I wondered if they hadn't got it wrong and taken me for a queen. Since then I've got to know my way around better and I can take it.' On the Marcus ranch they'd prepared her wedding: 'There was a little short-horned bull just like me, with a wreath of flowers. And Mademoiselle Chanel dressed as a naval officer, cap and all, covered with gold buttons.' Georges Kessel went with her, wearing a Rembrandt hat. In New York he burst out laughing when a French waiter at the Waldorf Astoria greeted Coco with: 'So here you are, Chanel!' Seeing her amazement, he explained that was the American way of doing things. She saw he was French and cut him down to size by calling him a deserter. 'I know, a boat came for you and you hopped over. I shall ask for you to be changed.' The manager explained they'd found a French waiter because they thought she'd like it. 'But it's not necessary, I've got a maid. Just send me someone polite – a Rumanian.' They did so the same evening. 'A sweet old Rumanian who set about doing the ironing. "Careful," I told him – "I haven't got many clothes." ' Fortunately she'd brought her tweeds; otherwise she'd have died of cold.

Georges Kessel acted as her secretary on the trip: 'What an alcohography!' And of his brother Jeff: 'Night-club literature. They were only happy at the Russians'. They ate the glasses . . . I was lucky to escape all that mess. It was just the sort of thing to charm me.'

Through the Eleusinian mystery of voyage and return, she came back to the rue Cambon. 'Money wasn't worth anything any more in France. So one had to work and try to get one's little flag flying again.' Her profession of faith was vibrant: 'My only dream is to get rid of the collection and escape.' Not to the isles of Greece, though. 'As soon as you set foot on a yacht you belong to some man, not to yourself, and you die of boredom.' Coco preferred the return journey from her hotel to her rue Cambon.

'One ought to change saloons occasionally,' she would sigh at the Ritz, sending an underdone steak back to the kitchen. 'Crisp salad, well seasoned. When it's lukewarm . . . ! And anyone who eats fried potatoes without salad hasn't any taste.' Schiaparelli was lunching at the next table, an old lady in black astrakhan. 'A holy-water frog,' murmured the fresh and incorrigible Chanel. She got two new five-franc notes out of her bag and gave them to the waiter. 'That's all they can hear: You have to speak the language that interests them, otherwise you might as well beckon that tree out there in the garden.'

She took an hour off for illusion: she was moved by the exhibits at the Musée de l'Homme, by the rock-crystal skull and fat granite hippopotamus. She hated totems, which she thought the world was degenerating into; the god Goult with his skimpy armour and thin legs reminded her irresistibly of a woman dressed by Courrèges. We wandered about among the human skeletons and skulls. 'I'd like to give a ball, with Dali, of course, and tom-toms.' She passed her ungloved hand over the stretched skins of the drums, to feel their tension. Backing away from an Aztec sculpture, she said, 'There, look at it now, it's much more beautiful from here. Things are like people: they can't do without their shadow.'

The eye of the camera showed up the grimaces, made huge the slightest quiver in the Japanese Olympic Games. Of the trembling lips of a black: 'Look how they breathe. It's an incantation.' After the marathon the exhausted competitors drank and collapsed. The winner didn't drink. 'He'd be lost,' she explained, 'if he tasted the sweetness of water.'

Her dresses became her outings again. 'When the work's there you have to take it. If you behave badly with your work, it behaves badly with you.' Just half an hour at Saint-Cloud? 'No, it would distract me.' A cinema on Saturday? 'I don't think so. I want to go in and look through some materials.' To Madame Hatami who applied for a job in the work-room, she said: 'With a physique like that I'll take you on as a model.' It was Pygmalion with his prey, a young animal tamed: 'And you can wear pretty clothes in the evening to go dancing. I'd rather Chanel dresses went out at night than that they just slept in the work-rooms.' She reminded her foremen: 'Don't forget we show the collection on the 28th. At the very outside the 29th. I don't want to bring out my collection on a Saturday when everyone's at Deauville.' Going slowly and pensively back up the stairs, she leaned down to explain to the head of the work-room: 'Now is the time when everything happens. I take away or I add. I shall undo everything.'

I used to find her amber with fatigue but the true virtuoso, taking shelter on her settee among cushions of black sheepskin, her boater tossed down on a review, among her walls of China engraved with the signs of thunder and instinct. The mere crossing of the threshold cleansed you of the dust of the streets. A friend asked why she hadn't collected pictures: 'Because I can't see them,' she answered. 'I like to look at a painting properly, and I didn't fancy going around the house with glasses on.' The truth of the body went with her in everything. She was fascinated by antibiotics and took a pink pill to do away with her sore throat. She fastened her skirt every day with a safety-pin to make sure she was comfortable after lunch, and only went back to the Ritz to sleep. She slipped on the trench-coat stripped of everything military, tucking the fine gold buckle inside the belt. 'Don't want to look like a midget . . .' The little naked black velvet dummies rose up in their independence in the mirrors on the long benches,

'She slipped on the trench-coat stripped of everything military,
tucking the fine gold buckle inside the belt'

stripped of their finery, ghosts of the deserted house. The slim imperious figure of their mistress disappeared among them as among a row of pages.

For her the cool night air could not conceal the dustbins of the Ritz. 'Sometimes I'm so tired that when I fall asleep it's like falling down a well.' But when inspiration spread its wings she'd be furious that the rue Cambon closed down on Saturday and Sunday. I remember her talking passionately about her foremen to the receptionist at the Ritz: 'Do they want to become tramps, then? They haven't even a tradesman's sense of honour. They don't realise they're working for their own good, to provide for the winter.' Sitting at her table in the 'Espadon' at the Ritz: 'Waves of anger surge over me when I think of it – these people who don't want to work. I'll sack them.' But she couldn't resist. After a couple of mouthfuls she rushed off to the rue Cambon to see if there was any mail. 'Mustn't fall asleep over the roast.' I rang and rang at the bell: no answer. 'He's as deaf as a post,' she said calmly. At last Louis, the old caretaker, arrived, grey as his uniform with its faded gold braid. 'I followed instructions, Mademoiselle – there was nothing for you, only business letters.' 'What!' she thundered. 'How do you know they don't concern me?' He showed her the wooden post-box, behind the phone, which he couldn't open because on Monsieur Tranchant's orders he hadn't got the key. 'Monsieur Tranchant is fired,' cried Coco, 'and his successor won't last long either. He's a second-fiddle, I won't have any dealings with him. I'll give them my ultimatum.' 'We'll fire him whenever you like, Mademoiselle.' 'I suppose you know we won't be able to show the collection? For the first time ever?'

The old man was shaken. 'What do you mean, Mademoiselle?' 'No, it's impossible. No one will do any work.' Here I started to laugh.

We went to the Tuileries gardens. Coco didn't have a handbag – 'You know I like to get rid of as much as I can' – and when we got under the trees she began to sneeze. I told her I hadn't a handkerchief. 'I have,' she said. 'I've got a pocket.' Two gents coming from the Jeu de Paume went by in their tight-seated pants: 'Couple of starvelings!'

Back in her room she opened her wardrobe to show me her mink. It was so soft it hardly looked like fur. 'A little woollie,' she said, and took her sable out of its cover and slipped it on. 'It needs a belt. A belt makes things less dressy. I shall end up wearing it inside my raincoat.' Her wardrobe was of the slightest: 'One shouldn't spend all one's time dressing. Two or three suits, as long as they and everything to go with them are perfect.' When asked out to dinner she said she had nothing to wear.

To the floor-waiter: 'Porridge this evening. But yesterday it was cold. It's only the milk that's supposed to be cold.' There was nothing left for her to do but go to bed. 'I could have had the best apartment in the Ritz, but I preferred to live in a garret. My three attics – one to sleep in, one to talk in, and one to wash in.' Her palm and her ears of wheat rested on the mirror; the rows of scissors lay on the white dressing-table. Her big bed with its clean openwork sheets was turned back under the pink light of old-fashioned crêpe de Chine lampshades. A Russian Virgin hung over the bed-rail. Her lions were everywhere: over the glass the one in the Douanier Rousseau's '*La Bohémienne endormie*,' and velvet pin-cushions stuck with hat-pins. Other hat-pins fixed postcards to the rose-pink screens. What floated out on to the garden was something like a rather prosperous little dressmaker's room. The bathroom was of another age, full of clean towels, touching.

Why live in a hotel? 'Because I don't give a damn about anything. You can eat when you like, you needn't go out if you don't want to. Slavery, having to rush to lunch at a regular hour.' With her, encumbrance was an obsession. 'Sometimes I can't even bear a blanket over me.' The only appointments she made were impromptu. 'I don't want to have obligations. Remember, if you go soft on your work you

'Her wardrobe was of the slightest . . . "Two or three suits, as long as they and everything to go with them are perfect." '

can't do anything.' She would suddenly decide to have lunch at eleven o'clock on a Sunday morning: 'I'm not supposed to tie myself down at this hour, am I?' Asked on the eve of a première if she was really going, so that a place could be kept for her, she said: 'Just drudgery! They take you there like a parcel willy-nilly. And you find yourself surrounded when you get there by the people you live next-door to.' She liked to be left to say whether she'd come or not at the last minute. 'Suppose you have a dinner-party in the evening and you're tired out after working all day. You're so tired you could cry. It does happen, you can't imagine.'

One Sunday she escaped to the country, at the Dons' place. 'They give you lobster and foie gras. It's two o'clock before you sit down to eat. They ought to give you soup to revive you!' Going past the NATO building, which she referred to as the League of Nations, she said: 'Pity they didn't put turrets on it – it would have been all right then.' Her spontaneity never flagged. 'Le Corbusier – awful! Houses on piles . . . A house is a cellar for putting your wine in. When I have a house I always get them to cook a ham for hours in brine with all kinds of vegetables.' But as to her house, 'I'm like a snail, I carry my house about with me. Two Chinese screens and books everywhere. I've never been able to live in a house that's left wide open – the first thing I always look for is screens.' She mistrusted all constraint. 'One should live within one's means. Otherwise there's always that extra thing bothering you. Never have a big house. Don't get caught that way. It always turns out to be a millstone. Never enough servants to look after it, and you have to find people to live in it when you're away – and they're as rare as a pearl in a mussel! A servant's a rarity these days. Your home's full of enemies. It's not houses I love, it's the life I live in them. Why should I care about walls? I don't give a damn for them.' But when she did bother to have a house, her senses all came into play arranging it. She would order sun-blinds. 'In lustrine, very ordinary, just black cotton – they're like that in

'I've never been able to live in a house that's left wide open –
the first thing I always look for is screens.'

the best English houses. Just a little blind you put up or down,
so that when you lie down to read at three in the afternoon
your room's nice and cool.' When I mentioned Moroccan
cloth made of raw wool woven by Debdou women in the
mountains: 'Don't bring folk-weaves into it for God's sake!'
She loathed bric-à-brac, display. 'Cut out ornament whenever
you can. Nothing's more beautiful than emptiness. Furnish it
well, with peaceful things. Houses are like everything else,
they have to have their souls made habitable. And a house
ought to be natural, it ought to be like its owner.' Nothing
bored her so much as over-organised sitting-rooms where the
cigarettes are arranged in a little box. 'Sofas where you daren't
flop down for fear of damaging them. Don't let the chairs
get worn out. There are menders – it used to be a trade. These
rushes, not the others.' What she liked was to pitch her tent
and her décor with it.

'Coco camps out.' The last make-believe house was her refuge in Switzerland, the 'little suburban villa' as she called it. 'Switzerland's so commonplace – what I like is the contrast.' She transformed a cottage into luxury; to overcome the poverty of the outside all the inside was to be of lacquer. 'Lacquer's my element. It doesn't hit you in the eye. I've bought thirty-two screens in my time, and I've given a lot of them away, but there are enough left to cover my house.' It was to have double walls, double windows, everything double. She didn't like combined bathrooms and lavatories, and had them separate. 'We're not celestial bodies! Modesty requires separate W.C.s.' I promised her cloves from Floris's in London, which she patronised in her youth. 'I'll eat them. They're delicious – they smell of geraniums. It's the little things that are important in life, not the big ones. And if you'd like a steel chaise-longue in the bathroom for when you don't feel like lying on the bed . . .' There was a fountain where all the neighbour's bees came to drink, and a swimming-pool, 'just big enough for rinsing this,' she said, lifting her glass of Riesling. 'I cleared everything out. I want two Japanese magnolias that don't smell, and shrubs, not trees. So that I can see them. A house is for living in.' It was all green outside with a lawn – 'I'll have turf brought from England to fill in the holes, like in the Faubourg Saint-Honoré' – and a hedge. It was a tiny garden, but when you glimpsed it through the screens it looked enormous. 'One shouldn't get tied by the heels to things that are expensive. One doesn't live on show. Luxury is liberty.'

The staircase was a meagre affair made of tin. 'I'll paint it black and it'll disappear into the atmosphere.' She also painted black the iron garden chairs she'd found at Comoglio's. 'In Switzerland they ask the earth for the least little broken-down old piece. Fantasy. Dealers always carry a piece of cotton-wool soaked in ammonia round in their pocket to see if the bronze is real,' she told me. Of her armchairs by Diego Giacometti: 'I'll add a bit of gold leaf to their Etruscan cruelty. They're too high off the ground. An armchair ought to crouch.' Then she announced: 'It'll be a house of iron, that can't be eaten up by moths!'

She loved the unusual. 'I'm looking for some things to take one aback.' One Saturday Hervé Mille took her to the store-rooms of the dealer Kugel. As she went up the stairs with the caretaker, pausing so as not to get out of breath, she told him: 'If you want to get on well with someone you ought to arrange for him to have a little "find" the first time he comes. That's the way to get customers. There are too many amateurs everywhere. Everything is a skilled trade.' The man explained he didn't know the price of anything. Monsieur Kugel kept everything in his own hands. 'Quite right,' said Coco. 'It's a passion.'

She was interested, searched round, looked at a superb Austrian eagle but made no comment, at chalices of Russian porphyry, at saddled horses of which the Mdivani brothers used to have whole teams. 'The last brother's rolling in dollars, but he sold the horses. People ought to keep their things. His house in Paris is inhabited by huge overcoats and an old painted Russian woman. Dreary isn't the word.'

'I don't feel anything Chinese here.' We went down to the basement where the porcelain was kept. Hervé pointed out a black translucent vase, but there was only one. 'Not quite a perfect set,' said Coco. Then he went into ecstasies: 'Oh, Coco, look in this case at this East India Company service!' 'Twelve thousand dollars,' said the salesman. Coco approached in silence: 'My goodness! We must be at the Rothschilds'.'

She was thinking of her cottage in Switzerland. She liked a boulle cupboard. She preferred Pompeian, light, Italian Empire to French Empire, which she said was bourgeois. But what she was looking for was 'something that hits you on the head, something that jumps at you.' We went away into the grey afternoon.

'I'm going to dress my house,' she told me. 'A steep roof and wooden balconies don't cost any more than a fur coat.

You know what my dream is? One big room where everyone lives. I like a house to be full. Otherwise all that's left is boredom.' She went to see it in the snow. 'It was a bit unreal. There's no linen in it yet – no life.' She had the camp-beds covered with the wild sheepskin of her childhood. 'My father gave my sister and me a very expensive present each – a mouflon collar. So I thought that wouldn't ruin me!' She asked her furrier to supply some for making bedcovers. 'I don't want eiderdowns and all that. You get hot, you throw it on the floor, and in the morning you have to clutch it back again.' She contracted for supplies of cut flowers, so that the house should always be scented with them. 'When the house at Roquebrune smelt of tuberoses they used to say, "Mademoiselle is back." '

But she only scented Switzerland the space of a sigh.

Her guests, Hervé Mille and Jacques Chazot, quarrelled and played cards. 'I still preferred the English week-end myself . . .' She crouched in front of the television watching Eisenhower's funeral. 'I could see how America has changed. After 1914 their processions were ridiculous – white shoes and yellow shoes that didn't march in time and made you want to laugh. But for Eisenhower's funeral they did things in real military style – it was as good as England! Two young soldiers carried the coffin – lead, because a corpse smells and it had to be paraded round. They lifted it up without moving a muscle. During the lying in state they didn't leave it alone a minute.'

Coco came back to Paris, furious. 'I don't play cards. It bores me, and I see all those faces wondering if they can catch me for a hundred francs . . . They were born with cards in their hands, and when they ask you to come and have a little game they mean come and get fleeced. My house is too small to hold packs of cards!' She never set foot in it again; instead she stayed at the Palace. 'I camp in Lausanne as I do in Paris. You know I never settle down anywhere. I've chosen freedom!'

The Challenge

Tear off, destroy all these vain ornaments.
RACINE

The Challenge

I remember Coco cutting bits out of a typed page of maxims she'd written and making them into thin strips for me. I watched the remains getting smaller and smaller. 'That's how you arrive at a text.' She exercised the same rigour towards human beings. The word was always on her lips, sinuous temperamental lips which belied the intensity of her glance and were always launching laughter or a piquant remark. Her rigour had far-reaching consequences: isolation, solitude. A diamond that cuts window-panes.

'I never tell a lie. I don't like living in ambiguities.' Her vulnerable eyes refused to bargain. She had her own truth. She tore it out as she would tear out a sleeve that wasn't right, pulling it to shreds. You didn't breathe incense or backstairs in her company.

'Colette preferred two grilled sausages to love. The way she ate . . . It was out of shyness. Once at the Princesse de Broglie's I stopped her at the twenty-fifth sausage: "Do stop, Colette, you're overdoing it and ruining your health." ' She'd made grub a substitute for everything. To her friend Patin de Polignac she used to say, 'Patin, my Bouzy,' in her drinker's voice, to remind him to pour her some wine. The rotund Colette called Coco Monsieur le Couturier and said she was too thin. 'I hate fat,' answered Coco.

Of academic speeches: 'Watching one starched gent perorate at another starched gent. Yours very sincerely, I don't think!' But one member of the French Academy that she admired was Jean Guéhenno. *Changer la vie* was authentic. 'The heel costs more than the upper – his father was a shoemaker.'

'It's been said I came from Auvergne wearing clogs. They

Coco in Venice at the Lido

don't know what clogs are. They're heavy. That's why peasants walk like ducks. Others said I was born on a stud-farm. Too chic for me.' When Louise de Vilmorin brought her the manuscript of her attempt at a life of Chanel, Coco cried: 'But it's a novel by Gyp!' Coco had 'taken her in' in Venice: she stopped going to the Lido, which she liked, because Louise didn't fancy herself in a bathing-dress. One day at two-thirty, after they'd lunched and drunk enough grappa to give Coco a headache, Louise went off with a boy who'd come to fetch her. Louise had difficulty getting round her: 'Lend me a thousand francs.' 'No, not every day!' 'But I've forgotten my purse.' 'What's the odds, it never has anything in it.' Coco dined with her and a man. 'Cocteau said to me: "But don't you see? It's her brother." Close as brother and sister, with a vengeance.' Louise was playing at incest.

She kissed the boy on the mouth and took things from everyone's plate and fed them to him. Her works left Coco unimpressed. 'Louise speaks Austrian. So old-fashioned. At the British Embassy, when the Duff Coopers were there, she fainted, and had to be put to bed. She never got up again.' Sometimes she used to take up her guitar and sing: '*Je me gondole dans ma gondole.*' The all too charming Louise sank in Venice.

Of Antoine de Saint-Exupéry: 'It was as if he was wearing a cassock. A kind of angel . . .' Coco never skimmed over, was never superficial: she who couldn't sew followed the seam, tracked. She made a face at the name of Marie Laurencin: 'Her mother was a waistcoat-maker – Marie did trousers and little girls: a bit of pink here, a bit of blue there. That's not drawing, it's just making splodges.' Coco ventured to touch up a portrait of herself by Cassandre which she found unrecognisable: 'I looked like someone drowned, with long endless Italian hands.' She scribbled over it to give herself some hair. Misia Sert congratulated her: 'I've just dressed it up a bit,' she answered.

At a luncheon-party in the rue Cambon she admitted: 'It was I who gave Cassandre his start. Then I shut the door in his face. But he came back through the kitchen.'

'He was in love with you, Mademoiselle,' suggested Chazot.

'In love with nothing – in love with money. Every man's hand against another for the sake of a crust.'

She leaned back farther on the settee like a sheaf on its withe. Was she going to yield to indolence? But the lightning flash soon came: 'Régine! It was you people who made her. Always after her, always there. It was all right so long as she was still in her dive . . . that was the proper place for her . . . but at Olympia . . . ! The Americans call her Boule de Suif. That just suits her.' Chazot said he was going to hear Elisabeth Schwarzkopf that evening: 'Schwarzkopf's a bit of a drag, but it's a beautiful voice.' She didn't let her wrath get rusty: 'And your friend, whose name I won't mention, who's opened that frightful club where people wear coats without any collars. A good clean sweep's what's needed there!' And when Chazot had gone: 'Chazot – he's not even Maurice Chevalier. *I'd* never have put up with being an also-ran. I'd have had to be first.'

She'd liked Gérard Philipe when he played Lorenzaccio, his face streaming with tears and so marvellously dressed. 'The effects he could get with his boots!' Her judgment was as accurate in the theatre as in society. She laughed, remembering the time Arletty came to dinner and said: 'Cocteau wants to write a play where I show neither my legs nor my ass. So what's the point?' Arletty called Antoinette d'Harcourt 'my duke.' The duchess had had her teeth straightened: 'They were too regular – a piano.' Coco was angry because she didn't bother about Arletty's financial needs. 'She's not a beggar, she's a woman who's had lovers. You've got some jewellery, haven't you?' The duchess brought a miserable scarf-pin. Coco lashed out. 'That's not a brooch, it's an orange-pip!' That evening she pointed to a diamond bracelet: 'Slip that on her arm,' said Coco, 'and if she needs money she can always sell it to a jeweller.'

She missed her insolent friend Arletty when the lead in *Madame Princesse* was played by Marie Bell: 'If only it had been Arletty instead of that great lump. I don't understand why she doesn't have it all massaged. She ought to give up wearing trousers. She always tries to be equivocal, in pyjamas and covered with artificial jewellery. Doesn't she realise a fortune-teller would wear a slightly out of date dress?' She couldn't bear Ludmilla Tchérina as Salome: 'She affects to be beautiful and graceful and a dancer, and she's nothing. And she's put on weight. It was flagrant enough in *St Sebastian*, but this Salome just beat everything. And she'd loaded all the dancers down with necklaces: Herodias was wearing a whole flea-market!'

Coco liked Richard Burton when he came with Liz Taylor and she said lovingly, in answer to a question, You'll have to ask number one. 'He got into the car before Liz, and she scrambled after. When she looked at him her eyes smiled. He looked at her with his mouth. He's working-class, you know – he stares at you as if he were taking your clothes off. He hasn't forgotten where he comes from – Wales.' She told him she'd like Liz to play Coco. 'She's too fat,' he answered, getting hold of her bosom in both hands under her silk blouse. 'Too much here.' Coco laughed: 'Liz ought to be dressed as a gipsy, not as an English lady of fashion.' She told him he was a terrific actor, and how much she'd liked him in *Becket*. The play she had liked less: it was Anouilh. He was touched; he was hot – he asked for whisky and for the windows to be opened. 'The archbishop is superb. I'd never seen an excommunication, and I went back four times to see what it was like.' Medals, chains, cults of all kinds enchanted her. Then the pitch of her enthusiasm for the Burtons descended a tone: 'They learn their French from Alexandre. It's he that gets them invited around.'

She didn't like the film about Falstaff. The king didn't look like a king. 'Orson Welles put too much lewdness into his part. There *is* perversion in that big fatty of a Falstaff, but there's grandeur as well. But it's not there when you look at Orson Welles. He makes it American; not English, not Shakespeare. Extravagant.'

When she met Charlie Chaplin she asked him how he'd found his costume. 'Bit by bit, backstage and in old-clothes shops.' She didn't waste time over the wife: 'Oona – what fertility! And apparently the daughter's like the mother.' When her Swiss lawyer, who was also Chaplin's, began to talk to her about his Autobiography, Coco said curtly: 'He should have stuck to talking about his work. You need talent to talk about your life.'

She remembered there were moments when Diaghilev would have liked to spew up all ballets and have done. 'Then he used to sing.' She went with him to hear the tenor at the Opera and discovered Verdi. 'Callas can't get near it. When she lost weight she lost her voice with it. The orchestra has to help her out. When her voice gives out it has to make an awful din.' Picasso called to take her to the 'hôtel Pleyel.' 'He goes about naked now,' she said wistfully. 'That's why he lives at Cannes – there's no need to dress there.' She adored bel canto. Once Caruso, coming out of the Opera with an accompanist, observed that he had a sore throat. 'It's because I haven't sung enough,' he said, and began to give forth in the street. Then, 'Quick, give me my muffler, or I'll be a baritone by the morning.'

The pop singers left her unmoved. A little wisp of a voice and they thought it could be helped out by a writhe of the shoulders. 'By next year they'll be dead and buried,' she predicted. 'Monsieur Adamo's left them behind already. This everlasting sham . . .' She sighed: 'All these mountebanks. As soon as they can wiggle their little finger they start talking about art! People with tiny talents bore me to death. The things that used to be bearable in the days when there was no gramophone aren't possible any more. Monsieur Rubinstein can play the piano better than just anybody. These women that think it's the proper thing to sit down and tinkle nicely at the piano – I'd crown them with it! The best thing to do is put on a good record and listen to all the masterpieces. There are plenty of popular songs if you want them.' She was still moved by Tino Rossi and his half-century of midinettes, but she preferred the melodies of Léo Ferré. 'Monsieur Aznavour making eyes – now his career as a singer's over he bets on looks.'

When Paulo Picasso, Olga's son, came to dinner, Coco talked of Dora Maar, showing her the flies Picasso had painted on the walls of her room. 'He saw flies all the time,' said Dora. 'What he saw was boredom,' answered Coco.

She loved wit. She liked the story of General de X, arriving at the Jockey Club, taking off his gloves, dealing the cards, and saying, 'You're all cuckolds, gentlemen.' The night before he had slept with his wife.

One evening, a gala at Maxim's. 'I used to get myself up in

'She loved wit'

my best for these things – as if there was only one day left for one to make one's reputation.' The gala for Callas as Medea left her equally cold: 'Druids – that's what everyone's interested in now. All these charities . . . I know – it's charity beginning at home. Society people stuff their own pockets.' Society got no change out of her. Edmonde Charles-Roux?

'The daughter of an ambassador setting up as an ambassador herself. Ambassador of *Vogue* maybe. Her sister's called Cyprienne. I said to her, "Why do you talk with that accent? – you're not Italian." It's as clear as the morning dew.' Coco hated presumption like the plague. 'Those people who say they're going to hear Karajan, not the music – I can't stand them.' She liked Karajan when he first started; he reminded her of a ballet-dancer. But now he dealt in exclamation marks: 'A mosquito darting about, casting a spell with each note.' She switched to the Bolshoi on the record-player: 'That's the music I like best.'

'The Russians are like nature – they don't know what vulgarity is.' They had charmed her completely. 'You never know with them. They're at the extreme, either of hot or of cold. At twenty degrees they're dead. They sing, and they weep.' She remembered the Archduke Serge, his finger shot off for a ring, and recited:

> '*Your eyes in the crowd know me not,*
> *But remember I have lived*
> *Through tears, oblivion, pain,*
> *And profound ecstasies . . .*

That's a Russian popular song. Compare it with the popular songs here.'

She was touched by *The Lily of Brooklyn*, in which the mother, a house-cleaner, read her children a page of the Bible and a page of Shakespeare every evening. 'Until they're old enough to read it for themselves. That produces people who are really intelligent.' She had an exclusive, intolerant sense of childhood: 'You shouldn't split children's ear-drums. They spend all their time with schoolmarms. You should speak to them seriously, let them take their own time and pace, not bring them up like trained monkeys.' She knew well enough, deep down, that children guess everything. The desire for truth in the raw, without the over-refinements which the violence of youth rejects before adulthood establishes its

Coco in fancy dress at a party given by Marie-Laure de Noailles

claims and categories, was natural to her. A link sprang up between her and children straight away. 'Leave your daughters to lie fallow,' she used to say to me. 'It gives a good harvest.' At Lausanne she met a little boy of six crying in the street: 'Come on now, it's not as bad as all that.' He stopped crying in astonishment: she'd spoken to him as if he were grown up.

She wasn't taken in by appearance, formality, masques and bergamasques. She went straight for faces, muzzling them with her own original yardstick. 'If my friends tease me for talking non-stop, it's because they don't realise I'm terrified at the thought of being bored by other people. If I ever die I'm sure it will be of boredom.' She made short work of coxcombs. To the lickspittles surrounding one patron, she longed to say: 'Be careful you don't swallow the plates.' Of Marie-Laure de Noailles: 'She inherited a taste for bargains from her father and has acquired some marvellous pictures. But her grandmother, Madame de Chévigné, told me, "She'll never know the sort of things that have to be learned." ' A fellow-guest suggested that perhaps the parasites lay in wait for her. 'And supposing she likes them?' answered Coco fiercely.

In her intoxicating *tête-à-tête* with life, liberty never lost its place. 'One should throw oneself into the fray, see everything. Some people ask what for. Better stay comfortably where you are and await the event. But if you wait there isn't any event.' Among the 'events' of May 1968 she advanced too, with her slim outline and scissors, iconoclastic as ever. 'I'm not going to stay at home shivering with fright . . . I'm as much of a rubber-neck as anyone.' She climbed into her long black Cadillac to go and see. 'And if anyone bothers me I shall tell him, I'm a princess and I spit in your face. It's not the students,' she told me firmly, 'that's only a front. I shan't start to worry until I've seen the infant schools marching in the streets shouting "Down with parents, up the kids!" ' She leaned out of the window and saw the children from the school nearby. 'We're in the rue Cambon, not at Le Mans. They should be moved on now they want to make speeches. I thought the young gentlemen had grown out of their satchels. But no, there they are, satchels on their backs, same little shrimps as before.'

Her protest came from another age and was a lofty one. But the burnt-out masks of all idols, even Brahmin ones, have the same ashes. She was the real 'contestataire.' She remained a 'boss,' but she was always recutting and adjusting the pattern of her life, which though foreign to most of our paths was strangely concerned with the destiny we all have in common.

Politics didn't impress her. 'Some people are like may-bugs. All you have to do is shake the trees and they fall off and die.' According to her you could only really make your way in politics if you kept your hands free. 'They've spent too much time with society people, where they only talk scandal and horrors.' Of the succession of ministers: 'Maids-of-all-work, as I've always said. They fit them in where they can.' She went to dinner with Françoise Giroud, where she met Mendès France. She warned him against a phenomenon, then as invisible as an iceberg, but which they were all going to bring into the foreground: Gaullism. 'I was waiting for everything to be red, for blood to flow . . . I expected lions,' she told me, 'and all I got were setters.' Servan-Schreiber told her she spoke as Picasso painted. But politics were not her job; she claimed the right to an opinion but no more: 'There's a chaos, but who has the key to it? Neither the one coming in nor the one going out. They're all on a level with one another – no one leads even by a nose. Everyone has his rival waiting. In our country they fight with words.'

She hadn't long to wait for 'General Yéyé,' as she called De Gaulle when he received Brigitte Bardot at the Elysée dressed as a hussar. 'I'd like to see De Gaulle go down the Champs-Elysées in chains,' she flared. But she whom Maurice Sachs compared to the Grande Mademoiselle during the Fronde could always see what was what. When De Gaulle retired she was indignant: 'I didn't like his politics – I don't like the military, anyway. But he's been badly treated! It's disgraceful. We behave like hooligans. If there was the least shred of manners . . . You don't just turn people like that out.' She was pleased with Nixon's letter inviting De Gaulle to America: 'That's what's meant by being young – to have reflexes and dare to act on them.' Toadyism she soon saw through: 'All those who used to kneel before him – not one rose in his defence. As for Edgar's tears . . .' And she declared one doesn't fight over a corpse that is still warm.

She told me De Gaulle's house at La Boisserie was very beautiful: a lot of grass, not very French, no masses of little flowers, but a big lawn that made you want to take your shoes off and walk on it. The reconciliation wasn't long in coming: 'That great romantic, wandering about Ireland heaving sighs fit to split the earth asunder.'

And when the general died: 'The Champs-Èlysées are full of people – the burial of the great is the entertainment of the small. Saint De Gaulle! they're in the process of canonising him.' She respected the integrity and modesty of Couve de Murville: he said what ought to be said, with dignity. 'And with a touch of shyness, which never does any harm. And wanting to weep. And also Couve is thin, whereas those big bellies stifle everything with their vulgarity.' One other won her support: 'Calm, organised, speaks well, level voice, doesn't shout, no theatrical effects, and he has a programme for people who work. If I was young I'd vote for Waldeck Rochet.'

She was resistant to the parade of the election. 'Always voting, I can't stand it! Monsieur Poher hasn't got the stature. A president of the Republic ought to be representative. *He*'s like someone without any legs. A president has to preside. The other day he was wearing a coat and you couldn't make out whether it was a frockcoat or an overcoat. He'd hired it that morning.' The Pompidous? 'I'll go and see them to-morrow if they crash. But if they're at the Elysée, don't count on me to be round there on skates.' One of the guests mentioned Coty: 'Who, the perfume chap?' Everyone laughed. 'But it's you who've got bad memories. He used to be the best perfumer – scents that used to be hidden under bobbles. There was a glassmaker at the time who used to make hideous bottles. It was then I launched Numéro 5. Madame Grès has a perfume called Cabot or Caniche or something like that – some dog's name.' Cabochard, no doubt. Coco had her taboos.

Serge Lifar came in, gold chain round his wrist, and announced in his incorrigible accent: 'I'm leaving for Cairo.' 'You've danced too much, old Serge,' said Coco. 'What!' roared Serge. 'I only had my body to express myself.' Coco's tongue didn't spare her friends: 'Friendship isn't for handing

Coco and Serge Lifar

round blarney.' Her sensibility and her exactingness made a strange couple, though no doubt the one derived from the other. 'One shouldn't speak of oneself, or almost never. People should guess you. If the soul issues forth anywhere, if it listens and talks, it's on the tongue. The mouth is our most sensitive part.' She hated soft-soap; minuets sent her to sleep; baskets of flowers had no effect on her. 'One camellia would have been enough.' Madame Esfandiary had been her secretary for a long time, and Coco said to her: 'Too many flowers, Esther. There must be a catch somewhere.'

The provincial in her always hit the target. Her way of talking was beautiful, full of images. 'The ashes are beginning to fall . . .' A young publisher in smoked glasses, who hardly knew her, asked her out to dinner and insisted on her having foie gras. 'These people who talk to you as if you'd never had anything to eat before in your life!' she said in astonishment. He rushed round to Guillaume's, where she was under the dryer, to present his compliments, which she could do without: 'It isn't as if we raised pigs together. These people are in for some nasty surprises.'

The Kennedys were her *bêtes noires*. 'America had become their property. The great joke was to throw you in the swimming-pool. If they'd done it to me I would have spat right in their eye.' Hélène Lazareff went into ecstasies over Jacqueline Kennedy's naturalness, crouching down with her children: 'You forget, my dear, that she had the photographer come!' Coco thought it shocking that at the inauguration of the memorial in London, Mrs Kennedy, instead of curtsying to the Queen, just walked forward and nodded curtly. 'But a queen's traditional!' For Coco, unpardonably, Jacqueline Kennedy was the quintessence of the little-girl style. She showed no surprise at her remarriage: 'Everyone knew she wasn't cut out for dignity. You mustn't ask a woman with a touch of vulgarity to spend the rest of her life over a corpse.'

When the Goudekets brought her back from Gérard Mille's house, where she'd been to see her friend on his death-bed, Coco found herself in the Baron de Rédé's car, a Rolls full of rugs and over-long furs. 'My God, where am I? A real prostitute's car.' Madame Goudeket offered to 'bed' her – 'What else? Her name was Sandra, a model's name, and she's Rumanian.'

Coco had known Boussac when he carried a remnant round with him under his arm. He'd become a gentleman and rushed up when she was at the weighing-in, though she preferred the paddock. His wife Fanoche had bows on the backs of her shoes, and sent her orchids with a card saying: 'A few flowers from my little garden.' Coco replied that her garden wasn't little, it was a park with hothouses and seven or eight gardeners, and that the orchids came either from there or from the florist's, but certainly not from a little garden. She said of Bleustein-Blanchet. 'He's the king of France,' and was astonished his drugstores didn't cover the tomb of the Unknown Soldier.

A lawyer was announced. 'He's a spy. They'd all cut their throats for Chanel perfumes. He's got a foot in every camp. One day I'll tell him: "You're riffraff." I know, because I'm riffraff myself.' She became a thunderbolt as soon as her independence was touched. 'I don't like lawyers or policemen or soldiers.' Ever since her wild adolescence that mocked at restraint, these people had reflected for her the parallel shadow of bars. The instinct of self-defence made her fight fiercely, lithe as a lash. 'I spend all my time wrestling. To-morrow they'll all rat. How I'd have fought when I was twenty!' Of her lawyers: 'Little kittens. Miaou, miaou, miaou. You have to spoonfeed them glasses of milk. Not one of them's capable of resentment or getting into a rage!' When she was with business men: 'I keep quiet so as not to give myself away. I mustn't let them see I don't understand a word of what they're talking about.' But she went to Zurich to see the one she called Methuselah. 'I always go to the top. I'll tell him: my pride mustn't be hurt.' She said she lived among usurers. 'But they'll make my perfume, they'll do everything.

Not for peanuts! If anyone asks me what two and two make I'll say: twenty-two because I'm a Jew.'

She nicknamed Pierre Wertheimer 'bonjour tristesse.' 'He was a generation behind. I used to tell his wife: "Make him wear a beard and he'll look just like a patriarch." ' The thing that amused him most was to see Helena Rubinstein walk round her bedroom on her hands. 'She was brought up in a circus. Anything so long as he bought her creams.' Helena Rubinstein gave a luncheon-party and interrupted everyone who made too much fuss serving her because she wanted to hear Mademoiselle Chanel talk. 'She almost rapped their knuckles to make them be quiet! The waitresses looked like nurses. And she had a face that looked as if it had just been boiled and was still steaming.' To Coco, who got up late, Helena Rubinstein said: 'I'm in my office at seven in the morning and I sever relations with any members of my family who can't do the same.' Coco sighed: 'She'd make a good house-maid!' Her lynx eyes weren't dazzled by the other's enormous jewels. 'They needed cleaning. Disgusting,' she said indignantly, neat in her pearls.

She had a horror of stars, which didn't help Brigitte Bardot much: 'Good proportions, but rotten shoes and rotten stockings, and her clothes come from here, there and everywhere. She still plays with toy animals – the level that implies!' Coco wasn't to be tamed by 'instincts': 'She takes us for Papuans! Disgusting, holding ducks and hens under her arm. The awful smell. So she arrives like that from Brazil with her quacking. If she was fifteen one would say all right, she's still a child, but she's over thirty. The child-woman won't do nowadays.'

In vain Chazot proposed Catherine Deneuve, Elsa Martinelli for Chanel's first show on television. 'Too nice, too big, tail too close to the ground, Italian. I don't want anything to do with that populo!' Her collection could be shown, the time-honoured number in the models' hands. 'But I wouldn't show my nose for anything in the world – it would be selling myself cheap! I'm not commercial and I can't bear that vulgarity. You want to make me like a little Monsieur Cardin, put me among the sort of people who give in . . .'

'But they're everywhere, Mademoiselle.'

'Exactly, but I'm not! No! I'm not the galley-sergeant of the Maison Chanel, worse luck for you. I'm Mademoiselle Chanel, a private person, and that's how I intend to remain.' All Chazot could get her to agree to for his cameras was: 'In the street. I don't mind that. Come and pick me up at the Ritz as usual.'

Pascal announced that Monsieur Dali would be coming to lunch the following day. 'Give him some game that's gone off. He'll eat it.' Then she changed her mind: 'No – have to think of myself – poulet à l'américaine.' She laughed, remembering the dubious restaurant Gala took them to once. 'What's bred in the bone will come out in the flesh.' Dali knew his friend. Every muscle of his moustache quivering with rage, he said: 'Give her something very white and clean,' 'Now,' said Coco sadly, 'he eats Lanvin chocolate, gets it all over his face, and tries to lick it off. And wears a lamé tie . . . This wretched little circle people talk about so much – I find it wretched.'

Cecil Beaton made her think of an elderly Englishman from the Bahamas. She hated the costumes in *My Fair Lady*. 'I wish you could see what Ascot's really like!' Instead of the 'English tramp I love,' she saw an awful crowd which shouted and shrieked and dressed all in buttons. 'That girl sets herself up in a drawing-room and says all the things that shouldn't be said and everyone swallows it.' When Coco arrived at Ascot she'd told Randolph Churchill that her article wouldn't say anything about the women who were all in muslin, their arms blue with cold. But the men all wore morning coats. 'I was like them, in a raincoat.' Cecil Beaton: 'He used to disparage me – he's an old lady who's got older but not better. An old maid who's committed a lot of mortal sins.'

On Sundays she liked to walk round Père-Lachaise, between the Lady of the Camellias and the grave of Oscar Wilde.

Pierre Reverdy, 'the last of her heart's passers-by', with Gala Dali at La Pausa

'His sex of gold, then of iron, torn off. That, and talent, was what made him live.' She went to see Jean Cocteau on his death-bed. But she didn't recognise him: he had a fringe. 'Alexandre has arranged him a bit,' whispered Francine Weisweiller. 'Got up as the widow Cocteau . . .' The one thing Coco was afraid of was dying in Paris. 'I don't want a couturière's funeral!'

Her friendship with Pierre Reverdy, the last of her heart's passers-by, was often on her lips. He brought her his poems shyly: 'Dear Coco, you're going to be chewing stones.' Her own secret austerity recognised its counterpart in him. He was severe only with himself, she told me; for everyone else he melted. But other people were afraid of him because he said what he thought. In the south of France Picasso called up his friend and asked him: 'How is it you're here and you haven't been to see me?' On the beach twenty-five guests were having lunch to the sound of a guitar, and the manager of the bar raised his big straw hat and called Picasso 'Maestro.' 'When I saw that beachful of sycophants . . .' Reverdy told Coco. 'But then Picasso spread out his arms as if to say, yes, there it is, but hallo, and Reverdy wanted to laugh.'

'You can't read it just like the morning paper,' she said. 'Once you've started on *Le Gant de crin* . . . I could give up everything because I haven't lived that life. Just to have written a few phrases that give food for dream.' He used to arrive at two o'clock, from his country train, to dine in the rue Cambon. 'He was a lofty spirit. Toads didn't fall out of his mouth.' Silently she leafed through the manuscripts he dedicated to her: *The Song of the Dead*. He had entered the realm of all the others she had loved.

The television, totem of to-day and to-morrow, waited and watched for her. There again she emerged solitary. During a boxing match she would gaze intently at the man with hammered eyes who was getting the worst of it: 'I hope the little chap gets up.' Watching Churchill's funeral, Coco, she had known him so well, discarded the clowning, the cigar, and the cognac as so many props, and was moved by the ceremony of old England: dignity doesn't go out of fashion. Where are the sentries at attention, their eyes lifted towards order? When the Bedfords were interviewed the acid voice of the duchess recounting chit-chat made her hair stand on end: 'I'm no scholar, I'm a perfect goose, and I don't mind if something's made up so long as it's good.' The only thing she recognised was the trees, splendid and immemorial. 'The one thing that's genuine in England is the trees. You're not living in a modern wonderland there. It's all been dead a long time. Life's stood still. It ought to stay like that.'

Coco fled from it, but the shores of England were those of her idyll, and the mystery thickened like a mist. Her eyes, which had contemplated the horizon so long, contained this mist and had the freshness of expectation. Near her her gilt servants, rising out of the clay, brandished torch or hunting-horn. But the travellers were no more. 'When I look at that screen in the evening, I see gates open and riders setting out on horseback. Weariness hits me through my eyes. I sit there, trying to see if there's any defect. When I've finished the collection I shan't be able to see any more, and I shall have to go somewhere and get my health back.' She wore her pearl cross over the red-currant braid of her little sand-coloured suit, as authentic and ordinary as herself; she put on her pelisse. 'I have to work to-morrow.' She went down the stairs, over the thick beige carpet with the cloth edges. 'So as not to fall. When I thought of it, all the cinemas had it within a few weeks!' The chairs in the salon were arranged in rows and empty. It was the time Coco hated most of all, when she had to go back across the rue Cambon to the Ritz, to the hotel room devoid of symbols, with the icon over the railed bedstead, the books scattered over the shelves, the window open on to the air of the garden: a young girl's room.

Solitude

Memories are hunting horns
Dying away in the wind.
GUILLAUME APOLLINAIRE

Solitude

'I've lived or staircases. On the last step I hung back. I was alone.' On that staircase in the rue Cambon which she climbed every day, I've seen the childlike ruses she used to keep someone from going, to hang on to them by the collar, to stave off the return to her unalterable, intolerable solitude. 'You've got some hard weeks ahead of you,' I said to her on the phone at the Ritz, the morning the collection was announced. 'What do you mean, Claude?' she answered. 'You shouldn't say things like that. What's hard is doing nothing.'

What was hard was going back to her white bed, maternal and smooth, at the Ritz – the snow of her solitude. But she had unflaggingly rejected alternatives. 'I've known giants. People full of faults, but who dazzled me because they carried in them a world different from my own thoughts.' Gradually they had disappeared. But she was as chary of newcomers as of the plague. She preferred ghosts.

'He protects me,' she said of the marble bust that looked down on the intimacy of her dining-room from the mantelpiece. It was Boy Capel's uncle, an English ecclesiastic who was converted to Catholicism. Tender ghosts. Her ruby, diamond and sapphire rings were always on her fingers; others, of gold, looked like wedding rings. Her fingers had grown thin; the rings almost fell off. The sapphire ring *was* lost: 'It didn't love me and it's gone – I don't care.'

To be loved. That was the need, the throb of a heart to which she would never surrender. 'I can talk to you about my shop if you like. About my feelings – out of the question. I find such language degrading. People talk like that in bad novels.'

But her talismans didn't desert her. The topaz the old lady

'I've lived on
staircases'

in Auvergne had given her swung beneath her blouses. 'I had it put on a chain and I wear it all the time.' No emerald ever drove it out. 'I believe in everything,' she used to tell me. 'Three steps instead of five. One ought to be a bit of a fetishist.' Her collection used to be shown on the 29th; her newest perfume bore the same number as her birthday, the 19th. 'We must kill number 5,' she commanded Maître Chaillet, whom she was torturing over this latest-born: 'It doesn't smell.' But *she* was fragrant.

'In old age, elegance and fastidiousness are a form of dignity. A young woman shouldn't be elaborate – it's so dowdy.' Coco reserved modesty for the body. 'It's the body that has to be free and easy.' She went to lay out Misia's body, and remembered the Russian custom of dressing women up when they are dead, to be kissed in church: the last festivity.

'I never have lukewarm feelings for anyone – I either love or I don't,' she told me, with her deep eyes. Sometimes, after lunch in the rue Cambon, she would curl up on the settee, pull her boater down firmly over her eyes under the lamp that lit the magazines, and sleep for the few minutes before the signal to begin again. She had the trained worker's ability to cat-nap. She would wrap you in her sleep, yielding herself to it like a little girl, carried away, then wake murmuring drowsily: 'Waiting, always waiting.' The telephone was ringing. 'I'll be down in five minutes. I was a long way away. I wanted to get through somewhere and couldn't.'

She walked briskly past the book-lined walls, between the lacquers of Coromandel and the portraits of little Dutch infantas, to her bathroom: a red Chinese corridor, a strange lion on a sixteenth-century rug, the crystal cluster of her dressing-table covered with gilt boxes, the white enamel of the wash-basin and bidet, the bottle of surgical spirit, the spotless towels. From the stairs the aura of perfume announced her presence to her white-overalled women.

'What a paradox,' she used to say to me. 'We're in a corridor that means nothing.' Did her pathos, did the emotion she

' "He protects me," she said of the marble bust on her dining-room mantelpiece'

inspired come from the perfection she put into that most perishable of all objects, a dress? She offered that perfection up to illusion. 'I think I've made some very pretty things, but you must tell me – when one's working one's too cut off to see for oneself.' The thousand fatigues were nothing: the work enchanted her. 'I hold my world in the palm of my hand.' Work resumed, she was in a state of grace, invulnerable. It made me think of Renoir, and the picture she'd shown me of him at the end of his life: 'He'd taken on that form – a bone that had to be carried about, Renoir folded up, an easel.'

I've seen her go up to dinner at half past eleven, singing *La Bohème, Tosca,* and *Lakmé.* 'The beauty of a voice lies in its unity – it should be all the same colour, not better at one end of its range than at the other. I adore this act: he's high, she's low.'

She knew women too well to be deceived: 'A woman is a force not properly directed. A man is properly directed. He can find refuge in his work. But work just wipes a woman out. The function of a woman is to be loved.' The winged lion of Venice shone in all its gold. 'Not to hurry any more to be finished work at seven so as to meet the one you love.' The Coromandel screens spread out their undeciphered signs, their dragons, human figures among volcanoes, flotillas on a lake. In their shelter she was confidential, a pomegranate flower bursting open: 'I would never weigh heavier than a bird on the man I loved.' Her eyes grew bare, seemed to belong to the realms inhabited by her hinds of bronze. But sorrow came on the brink of night.

'My life is a failure. Don't you think it's a failure, to work as I work, under this lamp? I've cried a lot. And if I've found refuge in dresses and coats . . . When you've lost those you adored. I'm a prisoner, I never go out to buy things I need. I just think of a comb or a brush I want, but it's too much effort.' Her nugget of gold, her collection, the yoke of work, were no use to her any more. Who could lighten her resentment?

'In old age elegance and fastidiousness are a form of dignity.'

'What you're doing now is paying, I tell myself.'

'Paying for what?'

'For always going away. There's nothing worse than being alone. Yes, there is: two people can be alone together.'

She used to say, 'There's nothing masculine in me.' She'd remained vulnerable. 'Intelligent women – I don't believe in them. Sometimes, once in a hundred years, a woman invents something to do with taste, or with cooking, which is part of it.' She had no high opinion of ladies who do nothing all day but titivate, but she loathed bluestockings. 'Poetry readings, classes in art appreciation, that's not my style at all. Always in the swim and in the know – just a babble and a bore.' She saw women's fate as looking on, not being committed. 'They should shut up. Above all not indulge in society chit-chat.' But what's bred in the bone . . . : 'You won't find me wandering about the street: you see where this roof ends. I don't care a damn for cornices. I only think about where I am: about demolishing.'

'Beauty is the date when you were born . . . Infinity and the tip of the nose!'

'After you're fifty you have to deserve your face.' Coco at La Pausa

'As for putting the bit between women's teeth . . . They shouldn't adopt aggressivity. It's their weakness that counts. Women ought to play their weakness, never their strength. They ought to hide that. I don't like athletes!' She knew that women who are happy always show their weakness, and hysterical fear of growing old aroused her indignation. 'Beauty is the date when you were born . . . Infinity and the tip of the nose!' In a documentary we went to see at the Pagode cinema, she admired an old Russian ballet mistress: 'What a lesson! One can dance with the hands as well as the feet. The girl, the pupil, looks dead. No soul.' As she knew better than anyone: 'After you're fifty you have to deserve your face.' And she would storm: 'Unripe fruit! I used to know a man who said you can't do good cooking in young pots.' A woman of thirty understands life and knows how to pretend.

'Saying no, in everyday life, is dreadful, disparaging. One ought to say "yes, but" . . . in other words play the fish.' To a girl who was getting married and asked her for advice: 'I'm not an oracle, my child . . . When you marry a man you should think of it as if it was your first child. He's very fragile! When he comes home harassed and doesn't like the sample of sky-blue wallpaper you show him for your bedroom, don't try to be in the right. You should never say no to him.'

The only thing she loved was love. 'A woman needs to be looked at by a man who loves her, she doesn't need any beauty parlour. But without that look she dies.' She leafed through the pages of Reverdy's *Toujours l'amour*. 'Solitude destroys a woman. She needs to be kissed from her hair to the soles of her feet, otherwise she's frustrated. *I'm* not frustrated, I've had lovers!' She defended passion. 'If you told me . . . I'd tell you, *colla la bocca*. If it gives you pleasure! Otherwise it's not worth tying yourself down.' And with her knowledge of the feminine heart, she added: 'One keeps one's troubles to oneself. If anyone had made my husband ridiculous I'd have killed them!'

The only untruths she allowed were those of affection. 'A woman has a right to pleasure given and received – it's neces-sary to her physical and moral health. Then she feels guilty towards her husband and tries to win forgiveness. Those are the best marriages.' To live a dreary reality every day, only dreaming of love . . . 'As the poet said, Musset, I think, no one knows himself till he has suffered. It's a nourishment . . . Suffering makes people better, not pleasure. The most mysteri-ous, the most human thing is smell. That means your physique corresponds to the other's.' Gala told her she was going with someone. 'The thought that there's someone who possesses you, who kisses you, whom you can receive, is the best thing there is. When she came in in the evening Dali was delighted because she was in such a good temper. She got her men locally – she knew *them* – not in a drawing-room! It's a great shock for a woman when she's no longer caressed by a man's look.'

The women, once the hunted, had become the hunters. We

live in an age of confusion. 'The mad twenties. It's the present that's mad.' She told me: 'If I had my life over again I'd base it on physical pleasure. It's a little bit higher up the scale than eating well, having a good cook – then you haven't got to worry about that side of things. It's there.' I see her now, drawing the centre of pleasure for me on the table at the Ritz. 'Men have it outside, with us it's inside. So it's more vulnerable.' She liked the story of the Mexican peasant who made love standing up: he tied his wife to a tree with his poncho, hooked one leg over a branch, 'and then, you see, it's all a question of presentation. Not flopped down in a bed. Even if you're not willing he gets pleasure from you.' Assiduous herself, she marvelled at the intelligence of the human body, of its saliva, its teeth. 'One shouldn't be passive – it's an active function.'

Her hand ringed with the heavy emerald signet, she lifted her biscotte to her lips. 'Of course, it's a long time since . . . It happens to me sometimes in a dream – a little dream and then I wake. Now now, old girl.' The falls in the night, the bruises – what else remains of her confession? 'A woman who's not loved is no woman. Whatever her age. A woman who's not loved is a woman that's lost. The only thing for her to do is die.'

But her defences remained strongest of all. One of the last evenings that I went to call for her in the rue Cambon, she said to me from her settee: 'If passion came in through the door I'd fly out through the window.' Her nostalgia was for tenderness. ' "When men were strong they were chaste and gentle," ' she said, quoting Rimbaud. 'Someone with whom one can be the smaller one, the littler one. A shoulder to cry on. Tenderness is strength watching over you. The rest – any Tom, Dick or Harry can give you that. I've always had a husband! But a dancing partner with his hot arms – I always deceived him.' She wasn't abandoned. 'If I felt something was getting its hooks into me, I'd think: no, I'm not having that. But in those days love existed. You went out to dine in all the restaurants, you went dancing. You came home like someone who'd been well kissed all night. To come home alone, empty.'

Some tipsy American women, stiff as bodkins, passed her table on their way out of the Ritz restaurant, quavering 'Ooh, Miss Chanel!' Coco looked at them with her soft imperturbable eyes, and gave a little nod, a greeting which both pointed and concealed her boundless scorn. The incorruptible pupils of the eyes under the arched brows were the only witnesses: she met any inadequate passer-by with a radiant smile, and her tongue took a rapid revenge. 'What they'd like is to die dressed like Marie-Antoinette.'

No finery was any help to her now. 'Let's go,' she'd say to me. What her reserve prevented her from saying was that when the time came to retreat fiercely to her room at the Ritz, no one was waiting for her there. 'I have the dreams of a child. I dream of the life I'd have liked to have.'

Often I would find her half lying, sadly, on her couch in the rue Cambon, in the empty house. 'I was born at dusk, and at dusk I always feel a pang. All the people who loved me knew I was sad at the end of the day.' Sometimes, by chance, there would be an unexpected visitor from the past. Once she got a photograph of a mysteriously beautiful young woman out of a drawer crammed with them. It was Roussy. 'The way she looks there, completely lost, is because she was full of drugs.' When Coco took her to Prangins she pulled up her sweater on the train and said: 'Sert's parting gifts.' He'd pinched her, furious that she was leaving. 'You should have seen the bruises!' Coco saw her die, and told me simply: 'She's there, in the vineyard, in Lausanne.' I'd have liked the portrait to stay there, in its independent grace. But she shoved it away, face down. Friendship had receded before the dusk. Coco herself never wanted to be buried.

She would have stayed glued to the television screen until two in the morning if she wasn't dragged away. 'It's a disease – at night my ass is like lead. I can't bear the thought of going to bed.' She emerged wistfully from the serial: 'It's ten years since I was kissed on the mouth. I couldn't bear to do it to someone I didn't like, and if I did like him I'd run away.' She threw her fur-lined raincoat over her arm because she was too hot, tied her cashmere scarf round her neck, and went down the stairs. 'I'm like a boxer – I protect my weakest spot.'

'A man,' she said, 'is only aware of the physical love he inspires. He doesn't give a damn about grand passions – he was passionately loved by his mother and he doesn't want to start that again. He wants to be loved for his physique, there's nothing that means more to a man. Their hobby is making love. They've got what triggers them off – what a relief!'

She was worn out. The maid, a vestal before the soap opera on television, awaited her, undid her scarves without meeting any resistance. 'If you knew the awful stage-fright I'm in. The day the collection opens I have lunch at the rue Cambon, take a Nopirin, and then sit on the stairs. After that I don't know where I am, my nerves give.'

And yet she had a marvellous innate gift for relaxation. 'I know how to be inert.' She carried over her sense of luxury into the way she tied her kerchief over her hair or the way she dismissed someone who was a nuisance. 'Order bores me. Disorder has always seemed to me the very symbol of luxury. I've lived in and by luxury, trying to convey to my contemporaries the exact sense of what it meant for me, repeating over and over that a thing is only a luxury when you *could* do without it if necessary, but you *don't* do without it. Luxury is a relaxation of the soul. It satisfies an aspiration even deeper than the need to act or to think. You can only compare it to the need to love. To be able to love what's simple is a great luxury.'

She said: 'We should be like the animals. All I do is lie down and sleep.' She didn't deny her Romany sloth. 'I don't give a fig. I'm as lazy as a snake, indifferent, a harem girl.' What she didn't give up was her cleanliness. 'You can smell negligence. Ugliness may be forgiven, but negligence never.'

Her mysterious sense of smell hunted it out. 'I've had experience with my models. I make a speech and give them a little present: soap first and scent after!' And there could be negligence lower down than under the arms. 'Last night I was so tired I said to myself as I came upstairs, I'll go to bed in my clothes and not bother to wash. But you know me . . . I fight with myself. If you let yourself go you're lost. I haven't got anyone to keep me in order,' she said wistfully. 'So I keep myself in order.'

I found her in natural shantung pyjamas and towelling mules, a silk muslin scarf over her curls – a gipsy, but a dazzling one. 'Come any time you like – we're not society people, are we?' Lunch was served in the attic, above the chestnut trees in the garden, by the little Italian waiter: the Krug well chilled, the asparagus served *à la vinaigrette* – 'No sauce mousseline, it's all flour.' Toast melba in a folded napkin, purée of new potatoes and peas. A little Gorgonzola and Gruyère, and 'good strong coffee.' The riots and the rumble of a Paris of strikes and unemptied dustbins had disappeared in the unchangeable intensity of her eyes. She fled banality as one flees falsehood.

Sometimes *she* would mutiny. 'The old fogies of floor waiters here – the time they take. Lot of old relics!' She wanted to make a change, leave the hotel where the maid brought her the veal and potato purée first and then sloped off for the asparagus. 'It's going to smell for the rest of the day,' she lamented. She burned some incense paper. She was ready for some unknown departure. After all, she was only 'in transit' – her definition of her quarters at the Ritz, adding that of course she was the guest of Chanel perfumes. 'My defences are covered,' she said – a slip of the tongue for 'expenses.' 'If it wasn't for that, do you think I'd stay here to be pestered by all these people?'

My nomad was off. On the way, a drop of cool Riesling on chips of ice. 'I'm drunk as an owl.' Then she murmured: 'I was very miserable last night, marooned in front of the television.' I often found her, touching in her solitude, sitting at her dressing-table and staring out blankly into the garden. Slender still in her shift, she would suddenly appear to me with the wrinkles of all the years above her bare arms. 'I've got the arms of a child – very unpleasant.' Arms which hadn't embraced. Her eyebrows not drawn, thin in her silk pyjamas, bows of brown ribbon over her fringe, she was alone with her eighteen-year-old heart. What she called her infantilism. 'I always went away. When I sensed boredom crouching deep inside me, I left.'

At night, too, she went away, in her dreams. Of her sleepwalking: 'I did it last night. When I was a child it used to happen all the time. I ought to be tied down when I'm like that. The fact of getting out of bed wakes me up. I give myself a good bash.' She got her maid to tell it. 'Mademoiselle tried to break the comb, then she turned on the hot and cold taps and washed her hands. She kept rinsing the tips of her fingers, and stayed there in the bathroom.' 'Don't touch me,' she said to Jeanne-Céline. Jeanne was the ghost of her old maid, buried at her expense at a family gathering. Jeanne's sister Germaine, who took over, was long known as Jeanne, and when Germaine retired, Céline in her turn became Jeanne.

The splendour and misery of solitude. 'It's a desert. There's no more love.' It was in vain she exhausted herself, washing, in those nocturnal rites. 'When I'm ill, all I can think of is washing.' The fever became a defence: 'It's the good microbes fighting against the bad.'

She took off her make-up with the corner of a towel dipped in cream. Washed herself underneath. Took her bottle of water out of the cold white refrigerator. The scarves were folded away, the jewels stowed under the chamois. 'I used to wear pearls, but you need to have someone to string them. The maid's gone, so the stringer's lost too.' Lastly she tied a silk scarf round her head, covering first her ears then her throat: 'That's all that's outside, all the rest is under the bedclothes.' Even in bed she protected herself. In the face shining with cream the eyes were two lonely black patches. 'The worst is the angst. It gets hold of you here' – pointing to her stomach. 'It's something from the mind that invades the body. I never let myself go that far.'

She sat down on her spotless bed in the light of the bedside lamp. On the table, the eternal little pair of scissors. She slowly cut each of her pills out of the plastic sheet, got the phial out of its metal box, and gave herself her Sedol injection. 'No, don't touch anything,' she ordered. 'I know where everything is. I can tell if anyone's been poking about in my drawer. The Grand Chêne pharmacy in Lausanne. The maids – they pick the syringe up in their hands after it's been sterilised. They're capable of spitting on it to polish it up.' She plunged the needle into the 90° surgical spirit. 'Nothing could live in that.' She shut the box, with folded tissues and a file on top, and an elastic band round it. Then said to me: 'One shouldn't live alone. It's a mistake. I always thought I had to make my life on my own . . .' From the bedside table she picked up the *Bhagavad Gita* and the '*Eterna Consolación.*'

For many years she'd given herself an injection to make her sleep, but she saw it for what it was. 'I'm in favour of medicine. We live in an age when one needn't suffer just for the sake of a scruple. But calm should be in the mind, not in your stomach or your belly. They're just substitutes.' I never saw her do the injection in haste, except when she was in the last stages of fatigue or when it was very late, though it was her nature to shatter the ordinary conventions of time. Sometimes I thought of her friend, the beautiful Countess Kutuzov, and her Russian childhood, when, surrounded by nurses and pillows, the girls would stay awake all night telling each other stories. The enemy was loneliness. Anything that staved it off was a good thing, even sending the maid to sleep by her nocturnal loquacity.

It took me a long time to realise that her injection was a substitute for love. One day at Roquebrune she went up to

Paul Iribe on the tennis-court to tell him not to hit so hard –
he was a Basque and used to pelota – he lowered his glasses
to look at her and fell dead. She couldn't sleep any more.
Sedol was her last defence against night – the ultimate and
solitary penetration. 'As soon as I fall asleep, even if it's only
for a minute, I dream. I'm never alone.'

She came with me to the door, her mouth dry, and moved
me by talking about her negroid nose and her still beautiful
face. Perhaps she ought to do something about just under the
edge of the eyelid, with its suddenly rearing brows. All her
being sparkled with the defence of that beauty. And, she
confided to me, 'I take that Swiss stuff to keep my hands from
swelling.'

I slipped away over the now colourless carpet, with a guilty
sense that I was abandoning her to bad dreams.

'To sleep at last, without bad dreams, to be frail and held
in someone's arms,' wrote Albertine Sarrazin, who leaped
over the prison wall. Coco had fiercely rejected any domination, but she was at the mercy of her dreams. The iron rail of
the staircase in the rue Cambon couldn't master the inner
delirium, the violent poison. Her unconscious revenged itself
and besieged her with errors and dreams. Even her scissors
were no longer her friends. She would cut off a curl, sometimes a piece of her pyjamas: 'They were spoiling things I
made.' Sometimes she dreamed she was in silk pyjamas,
dressing to go out. 'The trousers were unfastened, they
wouldn't stay up, so I stuck pins everywhere.' Her solitude
couldn't bear being alone. The maid would find all the pins
scattered in front of the mirror in the morning. Or out of the
darkness of sleep there would appear a train, with a scented
coach full of flowers and 'Coco Chanel' written on the side –
carrying a corpse. 'Very good for my public relations,' joked
Coco. As the vesperal Colette had said: 'Oh heart's dignity
that no one sees, how the hour of dawn ravishes you, seeks out
the chink in your armour, wrings tears. But the sob of weakness is conquered now. A sip of water has got the better of it.'

'Her books were a rampart' – here in the rue Cambon

Her books were a rampart. 'Yesterday I felt so gloomy I came home at five o'clock, ordered a bit of ham, and looked all over the place for Dostoyevski's *Diary*.' Her favourites were *Conversations with Goethe* by Eckermann, Teilhard de Chardin, and the unforgettable English novels. 'One shouldn't stay on the heights of serious literature all the time – it's too much.' One day when I brought her *Olivia*, which had been noticed by Martin du Gard, who had a permissive attitude towards abnormal relationships, she corrected this description of him by saying to me: 'You mean he dishonours women in order to honour men.' And she added, 'All that sort of thing belongs to puberty – the little birds singing in their nests.' She might fall asleep over a book, but her second sight continued in her slumber. She would start, hitch her glasses up on her nose, and come awake all lights blazing.

Her proud little head could not always command the co-operation of the body. 'I'm frightened at my extremities. Caught by the feet. My legs are red up to the height of a pair of socks. I wear boots so as not to have to think about it.'

What was my amazement one day to find her at the Ritz, on her return from a journey, ill and wretched. 'I had a fall, but when I got to the clinic in the rue Violet I asked for a glass of water. It was dirty, and the nun who brought it was grumpy – just the sort of thing I hate.' In other words she hadn't waited for any more, but come home and gone to bed, all in. 'It didn't hurt so much after I'd given myself my injection, and taken three Supponéryls in case I dreamed.'

I called a doctor. The X-rays showed she'd broken three ribs. 'I'm frightened of people, away from my own place and my chair and my few books.' Of the stranger who examined her: 'When I found myself naked and vulnerable before the doctor, I felt like boxing his ears.'

Unforeseeable modesty, never divulged. But one ray lit up the legendary intransigence. It came from marvellous America – she felt America loved her. She who was on guard against any indiscretion, any intrusion into her secret solitude, trusted Alan Lerner and Frederick Brisson to put *Coco* on on Broadway, and didn't ask to see the script. Would she go? She had a white sequin dress made. Would her obstinate shyness and reserve allow her to keep the rendezvous she'd always been afraid of? 'A musical comedy – it frightens me into fits!' She applied herself, though threatening to abdicate, to her collection: 'Mustn't let down all the people who've worked so hard.' Lerner, lunching in the rue Cambon, had told her he'd found his 'grail.' Coco's only comment on Katherine Hepburn was: 'What an athlete! Look at those shoulders.' But above all, the innocence of the Americans overwhelmed her. 'To be loved . . . When you're badly treated, America comes to your defence. America is the Salvation Army.'

Her inner nervousness followed the calendar. New York. 'Enough rushing about,' she said to me. 'If I go to America I'll go by boat. An English boat, one of the "Queens." They have a grill-room. You can take refuge there. Each time you gain a hour on the clock. And when you land, you've caught up with local time.'

But what about fate? A week before the first night, I arrived at the Ritz to call for her and give her Maurice Sachs's *Sabbath* which she wanted to re-read. Her doctor came out as I went in. Her right hand was paralysed.

She of the hands of prayer, the working-woman's hands, was struck there, made dependent. I found her in bed, her hand hanging down inert. I suddenly remembered her saying: 'The thing that takes longest to learn is the independence of the hands.' She was still fighting, explaining to the anaesthetist how the papers were hounding her, and how it must be stopped: 'Coco here, Coco there. Let them call me Mademoiselle, if they don't mind. We're not buddies.'

So instead of Broadway it was the American Hospital at Neuilly. She didn't cherish the memory of it: one afternoon at three o'clock she suddenly awoke to find a priest at her bedside. 'Too soon,' she told him briskly. One consultant followed another: she would get back the use of her hand, but it would take three months for the nerve to be restored. 'I'd sooner have typhoid than this.' While people were humming her songs in New York, Coco was raging in the hospital at Neuilly: 'This is the most expensive hotel in the world. You'd need to be a ravening wild beast to eat the food.' Kerchief over her head, she became a gipsy again: a slice of ham, a pot of yoghurt, and her colony of books. But the glasses weren't clean. 'You have to buy bottles of vinegar to wash them! And the dragons on duty get into a rage.' She was given a night-nurse who snored like a bugler. 'Imagine trying to make me live with someone there all the time. The person who can persuade me to do that hasn't yet been born.' She refused outright to have a private nurse. 'I'm not keen on women, they eat your phosphates. It's a bore having someone hanging about.' It was settled. Coco returned to the Ritz.

I found her battling with her underwear. Céline had gone on a cure and she had no maid. 'They found a woman to replace her, but it was someone very queer, like an old man.' The knob on her television was broken, and I suggested telephoning to the housekeeper to have it seen to while we were having lunch. 'Not now. You mustn't ask people to do things when they're hungry. They're in the middle of lunch – it'd be like trying to tear their hearts out.' She reached for her bottle of Schoum Solution, 'for liver, kidneys and bladder,' and drank a yellow spoonful which looked like a child's cod-liver oil. 'I'm going to the rue Cambon in a minute,' she said. 'It's my means of defence.'

With a gold and black elastic band supporting the wrist of her lifeless hand, she started to work again. 'It was then I realised my staff were fond of me. They acted as if they hadn't noticed anything.' Serge Lifar told her about a healer he knew of in Sweden. 'Send for him right away,' she ordered. She was still at the stage of Madame Blavatsky, a Russian peasant. The healer came to the Ritz, sang the whole of *Pagliacci* in the Psyche salon, and kissed her hand but didn't bring it back to life. Coco told Serge to see to it he was properly taken care of 'so that we don't look stingy.'

It was going to take an implacable three months. She struggled every hour. Her fork slipped out of her fingers once, twice, several times, but she made herself persevere. 'I ought to play the guitar.' She'd never been made-up by anyone else in her life, but her hand was all over the place and she had someone come in to do it every morning. 'I make myself up for my staff. All the women who wait on the stairs and make room for me to pass: "Good morning, Mademoiselle, I hope you're well." "Yes." "Yes, you're looking well." '

She felt weary, battered, out of sorts, as if she'd been beaten in a hard fight. I tried to send her a masseuse who was very well thought of: 'An idiot,' she said. 'No, once you start letting people like that in on you you break up in no time. A woman who sticks her nail in your toe and asks you can you feel it! Fortunately I can! I'll have the beauty parlour round, but not that.' Her legs had become as slim again as ever. 'It's my manicurist – she gave me some Rap ointment.' That was the sort of medicament she liked. 'One must get as light as possible. Never let anybody else do anything you can do for yourself.' She tied a white muslin scarf in a turban round her head, to keep her hair unspoiled for work. 'You have to be well groomed and have your hair properly done in order to deal with rows. "The doors are wide open, if you're tired go and have a rest." ' It made one think of Colette: 'She is impressive as a cat, which only confronts danger well sleeked and ready, claws trimmed.'

Every Monday she set out to do battle: 'I'm off to cleanse the Augean stables.' All the truants of the week-end had to run the gauntlet, including her secretary Lilou, who'd been sacked so many times she'd lost count. But her animal charm and silent presence calmed her despotic mistress. One day when Lilou waited for her to get out of the lift at the Ritz, so anxious was she to be taken back, Coco said to her simply: 'I'm not d'Artagnan and you're not Athos or Aramis.' And Lilou came back and had lunch again in the rue Cambon.

Holidays, including Christmas, were her aversion: 'Stinking holidays. You need to have children. On New Year's Day I stick in bed and devour the sheets.' The season's greetings . . . I found her with a rose from Lifar, a tuberose from Dali, a bunch of red roses from Wertheimer, an orchid from Hervé Mille. He'd sent it despite the fact that they'd quarrelled, but she was implacable: 'I shan't let him come and see me till he takes back the letter he wrote.' Friendship? 'Friends. My friends. One doesn't have friends. Women don't have friends. Either they're loved or they're not.'

She suspected everyone, revenged herself for what people got out of her. 'What a mafia! They talk about what they call honour, but they parked their behinds on it long ago. They'd do better to talk about profit. There's no such thing as friendship, only money – not the same thing. Blackmailers are the people who are looked up to. I don't give in to blackmail and I never shall. I'm being punished.' She preferred simple people. François, her waiter, had become her manager. 'There's nothing more awful than being a servant: imagine giving someone a job, and the job's that of a servant! I try to help them rise above that, I try to teach them a trade, I can't help it, something makes me want equality, makes me have to help them climb.' She liked the peasant in François. 'He makes me feel peaceful,' she said. 'You know why. He doesn't say anything. What would Mademoiselle like to eat? The same as yesterday.' He was her bodyguard. 'What touched me very much was when he said: "I'll send Mademoiselle to Cabourg, to my parents'. I know Mademoiselle doesn't like the water, so it'll be a nice dry spot. And then I'll get in touch with her family to find out where Mademoiselle is to be buried." '

François came from Cabourg, from the seaside, she told me. She teased him about it: 'It's not really the country any more. It's been ruined by people on vacation.' He was the one person she trusted, and it was the worst form of betrayal when he married. 'I'm going to watch out now – there's a wife in the background. A different kettle of fish altogether.' I can see her now in her blue working skirt pleated in front, gold-buttoned cashmere cardigan over a white blouse tying loosely at the neck, and a chain round her waist, over the cardigan. 'I'm not hampered anywhere, not tight at the sleeves.' But she stared at the trays of jewellery for which she'd made François responsible. 'The jewellers can't come and see their work because Saturday's the wife's day at home. How feeble!'

On Sunday Coco was alone in the world. She never telephoned anyone. Only her rages spoke for her. 'You ring at midday to ask if I've got any plans! Are you mad? – Do you think I'm going to stay shut up on a day like this?' Through the torrent of insults I saw she was on her own and inviting me to lunch.

I found her sitting, getting ready, at her dressing-table. Céline handed her her stockings. 'You give me new stockings every day. What for? And there's a thread gone – more carelessness. Why do you do it? Give them to my storekeeper on Monday – I'm not going to spend my money on that sort of thing. They've got seams underneath to start with. And you're quite prepared to laugh at me going out with a torn stocking. A maid oughtn't to go around with nails that length. Everything's allowed to go to rack and ruin, when it all ought to be polished and seen to. Mediocrity that reeks of mediocrity! I have to get up and wash my glass because I can't bear dirt. A nice thing.' She soon cut short servants' gossip: 'If you were to tell me of doings at court . . .'

We finally managed to go down, after she'd fastened her necklaces and tied her navy and cyclamen silk scarves over her beige tweed suit. Monsieur Ritz rose to give her 'her' table, not in the 'Espadon,' but by the window. I thought she preferred this spot out of independence, but it was because she couldn't bear the smell in the restaurant at this hour, after everyone had eaten. Her eyes were intense, watchful. She sent the knives and forks away, saying they weren't clean. Monsieur Ritz was standing there. 'You see,' she said to him with a radiant smile, 'I behave just as if I were at home.' She told me the most awful, ugly, middle-class thing there was in France was a knife-rest. 'It's supposed to keep the cloth clean, but think of all the other dirt they don't bother about. And you need to have plates the proper size. In France they're always too small. The best thing is to buy them in England – white ones.'

'What's on to-day?' she asked the waiter. Some canary-yellow jackets, obviously from across the Atlantic, passed by. To my amazement I heard her say: 'I like those. I always told Alexandre a man shouldn't be noticed for what he wears.' She liked American menswear. 'It's stupid and old-fashioned for a man to look like an elderly Englishman. America's a young country that dresses ready-made. They just have to get into their clothes and take care of themselves . . . As for us French,' she sighed, 'we eat like navvies.' A fat lady in an imitation Chanel hurried by. 'Insignificance in forty volumes!'

The evening before, as she was going into her hotel, Coco thought she saw a man who was drunk stumbling over his

woman companion. He was paralysed. 'He must have wanted
to have dinner at the Ritz. He was in a dinner-jacket, very well
turned out; she was in evening dress. She stood in front of
him and put both his arms round her neck, and they walked
like that, she holding him up. She signed to the hotel people
not to help her. I would have run to go with them at the least
sign. But she didn't make it. And when the woman's hand
went near the man's lips, he kissed it. They were a happy
couple. They didn't need anyone.' Romantic Coco. 'There's
more than just bed. For Frenchmen that's *la porqueria*. If
I had to end my life living with a man, I'd insist on his
being English. Englishmen have feeling, Frenchman have
depravity. It's rather difficult to be romantic in an age like
ours.'

What sorrow! I quoted Maeterlinck: ' "If I were God, I'd
have pity on the heart of men." ' She replied briskly: 'I'm afraid
it's no use applying to God for that.' The Ritz was deserted.
She asked if there was racing that day. 'Yes, at Vincennes.'
'And,' she added, 'people have started going to Deauville.'
She liked to pretend she was in the country, visiting Sunday
second-hand dealers. After we'd driven through Ville-d'Avray,
she remembered she'd met Matisse there. 'What was he like?'
'Like all real artists – you didn't notice him.' The park at
Saint-Cloud reminded her of the rides Louis XIV's brother
had cleared so that his brother should come to see him. 'The
Sun-King was jealous.' Coco would have liked to stay the
week-end in the forest she loved. 'We didn't have forests at
home.' But the manageress of the hotel said, 'No, Mademoiselle, it isn't suitable for you.' It was a maison de rendezvous.
Coming back through the Bois de Boulogne she said sadly:
'There used to be men who played polo madly all day,
reeking of horses. That's all over now.' It was I who felt cold
in the car, and unfolded the light English cashmere rug.

I left her lying down, the air from the grey garden coming
in through the window, the incense scent drifting. 'If there
was a dog he'd jump straight up on my bed.' The television

screen lit up. 'If you feel miserable, come back,' she told me. She started to watch the tiercé.

Coco loved horses. 'I don't go to the weighing-in, I go to the paddock.' To smell the fresh grass, share the start, with the thin gaiters, tense sinews, the slender legs flying off from the starting gate. The finish, with the winner leading by a nose and the jockeys standing in the saddle, shaking one another by the hand, intoxicated her. 'I didn't buy my horses, I bred them. We couldn't keep Romantica doing nothing, so I had her have little ones.' Romanesque, Mademoiselle de Staël, Monsieur François, and Mademoiselle de Lespinasse were all offspring of her mare. She was indignant at the idea of letting horses be named by stable-lads: ' "Chanteuse de charme" – how could anyone stick vulgar names like that on animals?' One day, happening by Saint-Cloud, she went in and sat on

'Her heroes were solitaries'

the grass and saw her own colours. 'They've stolen my colours
... That red ...' It was Romanesque. She did the last hundred
yards with him. He won. She went to see him, puffing like a
whale and being rubbed down with camphor. 'The lads are
kind, he liked it, he was pleased at being rubbed down.
They're nicer than human beings, horses.'

Rugby, with jersey struggling against jersey, intoxicated
her. 'I could watch it for hours. They're men, and they're
really fighting.' The goal-line, the open scrum. I can see her
now, dining with her Swiss lawyer in the middle of her
collection, head drooping under her straw boater, hiding the
reserve of the granite eyes which no longer lit up at travelling
tweeds, ready to drop with fatigue. She came to life when the
athletes appeared on the television screen, running. A black
athlete flung out his limbs, relaxed, watched cautiously.
'Look,' she said. 'Just like an animal.' She predicted his
victory. 'Those who save themselves up don't win.'

Her heroes were solitaries: she loved Ludwig II of Bavaria.
'Wagner, Cosima. Dying strangling the other man – drowned,
though he swam like a swan.' Malraux's broadcast about the
return of Napoleon's ashes made her shudder. The French
wanted 'Napoleon' carved on the coffin at St Helena; the
English would only allow 'Bonaparte'; so they put nothing.
So when the survivor of Wagram cried out, 'The Emperor!'
and the door of the crypt of the Invalides was opened, what
went in was a coffin without a name.

'When I'm in my little coffin ...' The idea of heart trans-
plants made her angry. 'It shows the body still has a soul,
the fact that it rejects it.' Rejection, that was her vibration,
her soul, the fear of which she'd never rid herself. Her
nucleus of independence had become a zone of darkness and
cold. 'The only time I hear my heart now is on the stairs.'
She tugged furiously at the string of life, insisting on obedi-
ence, the cruel parody of love. But the Fatal Sister waited on
the other side.

'I don't believe much in death,' she told me. 'The soul

departs: the ordeal has lasted long enough. For the Hindus it's merely a transformation.' The Bhagavad Gita of her first love was still with her. Teilhard de Chardin wrote: 'We are only dust that moves and is transformed. It is the soul that holds everything together, and when it leaves us, the dust falls back again.'

' "Give up one's soul to God" – I like that expression. I'm a believer, but I don't see God the Father with a beard. What remains of us is what we've thought and loved in life. The life one leads is always unimportant. The life one dreams, that's the great existence, because one goes on with it after death.'

The poetry of Emily Brontë found a kindred spirit in her. Where would she go? To the wounded mountain of Lawrence's Princess, with its forests of cinders whose heaped-up trunks are only a handful of dust returning to dust? 'I don't like the mountains. I'll go and see the Rockies when I'm rid of this' – flicking at the lapels of her jacket – 'this miserable old rag. Then my soul will fly to the Rockies in travelling dress.' Had she recognised her likeness in the Princess? 'She wanted warmth, protection, she wanted to be taken away from herself. And at the same time, perhaps more deeply than anything, she wanted to keep herself intact, untouched, that no one should have any power over her, or rights to her. It was a wild necessity in her that no one, particularly no man, should have any rights or power over her, that no one and nothing should possess her.

'Yet that other thing! . . .'

The Enigma

Truth has no bounds.
COCO CHANEL

The Enigma

'People's lives are an enigma,' she used to say to me. The only roof Chanel recognised over her head was the fifth constellation, which contained her sign, the Lion. 'I love everything that's up high: the sky, the moon, and I believe in the stars. I was born under the sign of the Lion, like Nostradamus. I'd rather have a touch of the invisible than roast mutton every day.' Above all she preferred it to the family: 'I don't like the family. You're born in it, not of it. I don't know anything more terrifying than the family.' Dusk, the hour at which she was born one 19th August, filled her with anguish. But she had retained her childhood: a mysterious ligament bound the two together. 'Childhood – you speak of it when you're very tired, because it's a time when you had hopes, expectations. I remember my childhood by heart.'

Every life contains a secret. 'I was an unhappy child.' There, far away, was Mont-Dore, the centre for chest complaints, and the silent house where the children were told not to make any noise. Her mother was dying of tuberculosis: handkerchiefs stained with blood. Coco heard her little fatal cough, the footsteps of her father in the corridor, the people saying 'It's the lungs – she can't last long.' The little girl, left on the threshold of her mother's room, was sent from door to door. She and her sister Julia, whom she called Juju, were kept strictly isolated to avoid infection. Their father would pass through as they were having lunch and kiss them on the head. 'He hated the smell of hair and always asked how long it was since we'd had ours washed. "Three days ago, with yellow soap." ' The horror of hair was one of the things that survived from her childhood.

'My sister and I had tricoloured hair.' Their golden, chest-

The Enigma

nut and dark locks mingled with the purple and red black-
berries of the sunken paths they vanished into on the Thursday
half-holiday, a donkey carrying their lunch in a pannier. Juju
sang, they slept in a meadow and came home stained with
whortleberries. Coco was convinced she was drinking wine
out of her bottle of sugared water and little grapes. Her father
and grandfather were both Nîmes wine-merchants; phylloxera
hadn't yet attacked their vineyards. The little girl was of good
stock: her grandfather had a will of iron, and he fathered
nineteen children. He was as jealous as a tiger, and had scenes
with the little grandmother, her hair in braids round her head,
while the children listened to him thundering from behind

the doors. At table on Sunday they would eat their lunch and sit wide-eyed in their tight starched collars, watching him dispatch his daily marrow-bone. But that didn't appease all his fury: one Captain Dreyfus made him lose his temper, and he hurled the steaming leg of mutton into the garden, over his little grand-daughter's head. There was a dull thud on the lawn: 'Long afterwards,' said Coco, 'every time I heard a pheasant brought down in Scotland . . .'

The English used to come to gargle at Mont-Dore: the two little girls called them the 'Angliches.' 'I always remembered how the Englishwomen wore tartan in those days.'

'My father spoke English – that was considered something diabolical in the provinces.' He was gay and frivolous, and came from Pontex, near Nîmes. His name, Chanel, meant 'canal,' and Coco used it all her life. She never knew her mother otherwise than ill in bed. People used to tell Julia, 'Look after your little sister,' but once they got outside the garden gate they went separate ways. Coco used to go to the cemetery, and give the dead everything she'd been able to find in the house. She dug a hole and buried it: a little spoon or penholder whose disappearance caused a row. Her sister said: 'Follow her and see where she goes.' Coco remembered her father had brought her back the penholder as a present after a trip: it was made of knuckle-bones and if you looked carefully into the glass you could see Notre-Dame on one side and the Eiffel Tower on the other. Sometimes she would go looking for a nectarine among the vines, which she would put into her mouth whole: 'People said I looked like a nectarine, so I used to think, I'm eating myself.'

'I didn't so much love as want to be loved. So I loved my father because he preferred me to my sister. I couldn't have borne for him to feel the same about us both.' She used to recite Musset to him:

'*Poète, prends ton luth et me donne un baiser.*'

Her father roared with laughter.

When her parents went to La Bourboule, Coco refused to eat. Youyou, her mother's old nurse, was left to look after the house, which was ruled over by the mother's foster-sister, the beautiful and buxom Antoinette. 'My sister was six years older than me. She was sensible, and didn't see anything.' Coco hated the servant and said she was poisoning her. 'I knew she slept with my father – that is, I didn't know, I didn't understand anything about that sort of thing, but I guessed, and I used to frighten her by saying I'd tell my mother.' She and her sister set out on foot and went over four miles before, exhausted, they got a lift in a cart. When they got to the hotel, Coco fell asleep on her father's shoulder. The next day they bought her a blue dress which she wore as if she was a heroine.

At night she used to shake in every limb for fear of ghosts and the dark. 'Don't be frightened,' her father said. 'No one's going to hurt you.' She said there was a man under the bed throwing corn at her. 'But corn's very good,' her father told her, carrying her in his arms. She always had some corn with her after that. There was some in her attic at the Ritz, with the palm that was another relic of her childhood.

One morning the little girl could tell from the sounds in the corridor that her mother was dead. She and Julia went to kiss her on her death-bed. Funerals are a kind of party in the provinces. Her mother's cousins came and offered to bring up Jeanne's younger daughter. Coco was six. Her father took her to the cousins'; her sister was sent to a convent. He sold everything and left for America.

'My aunts? I don't even know if they had any teeth – they didn't interest me.' They were spinsters. There weren't many men about because there'd been a war, and anyway it would have meant breaking up the family possessions. 'I was brought up among women.' There was no breath of affection in those austere breasts. As they say in the Auvergne, the aunts were untilled fields. Pews in church, consecrated wafers, a house

'She always had some corn with her.' Glass table mounted on a sheaf; ears of Russian corn above brought back from Moscow by her mannequins

scrubbed and polished from top to bottom – these do not make a childhood.

There wasn't any shortage of food, though! 'Two old Midases,' Coco's grandfather called the aunts. The farmers gave them half of their perishable goods, together with turkeys and pigs. There was no refrigerator, but things were 'kept' in a big cool pantry. 'Black pudding! I'll take you to a place off the Avenue de la Grande-Armée . . .' One evening during the collection in which Chanel had dazzled Paris, we went to Camille Renault's at Puteaux for some black pudding. Apart from that, pork was forbidden: her father said it wasn't good for children's livers. 'I think the reason I've never got fat is that I don't eat pork.' Her youthful figure still stored her father's order up like a treasure.

When she got to her aunts' she said she didn't like eggs. She wasn't given them any more. But when she was tempted by a brandy omelette, her aunts would remind her of what she'd said, and she wouldn't touch it. She couldn't eat a mouthful of bread at the table, but would slink into the kitchen and hack off a huge slice of rye-bread. The cook would laugh: 'Coco, you'll cut yourself in half!' Coco had a secret code for communicating with the cook: two crosses meant I like you, three meant you get on my nerves. She loved the local wine: 'I used to go down to the cellar and have a little swig in secret, and I made the maid drink a big glass. "But Mademoiselle – " "No, go on, drink it all." ' There were hoots of laughter which weren't very much approved of, she told me, putting on an air at once apprehensive and irreverent.

The brass shone, warm home-made rolls were wrapped in white napkins, chestnuts sputtered in the embers. The Issoire peasant girls, shivering in their winter cloaks, hoods down over their ears, used to fill their pockets with roast chestnuts to keep their hands warm. Not a hair strayed from under the maids' white goffered caps. They dipped the dimity petticoats, tuckers and drawers in the wash, and rinsed them in running water. The big copper for boiling the sheets was stoked with coals and scented with strings of orris-root. 'The maids stretched the sheets – only the top sheet and the open-work were ironed. And the linen cupboards!' They smelt of verbena and rosewood. Draconian cleanliness was the order of the day. 'That's where I learned luxury . . .' She loved the smell of ironing and used to throw in an extra handful of starch when the maids weren't looking. It was in the wash-house, in the blue steam-filled air, that she learned about reproduction. The laundress hid her 'accident' under her white overall, and the little girl got the maid to tell her what the accident was. She explained as she folded the clean linen . . .

The favourite local girls' names were Anaïs, Françoise and Victoire. Aunt Anna was furious if anyone called her Anaïs, as if she were a maid. 'There were maids everywhere. Farmers' daughters. At 15 they had their hair cut, had a cap put on their head, and came to work for three years at 15 francs a year plus the wool to knit their stockings. They grew up – they could eat all the meat they wanted, but they got tall instead of fat, they were still young and fresh. Then they would leave for Paris. My grandfather had an expression to describe prostitutes: he said they sleep around like a maid without a situation.'

The picturesque language of that redoubtable grandfather still echoed in her southern ears: 'You look as if you'd put cuffs on a trout.' Of Pierre Chanel, the first martyr of the South Sea Islands, a Marist who was eaten by the natives, he said: 'All he had to do was stop at home.' Every year he used to give Coco a five-franc piece. 'I believe in a good year I might have had ten francs in my money-box. But I had to give it to the missionaries.' Occasionally she would acquire a marble. 'For a few weeks we'd go round with a little bag of marbles on our wrist. For us that was huge wealth.'

When the children played pétanque the boys always won: the girls' thumbs weren't strong enough. 'When everyone was very busy you knew one of the animals was having young somewhere, a cow calving. When the vet came the baby was already born and the only thing to do was give the vet a meal.'

'I acted as midwife to a little dog. She had four puppies. I stayed with her all the time. The feverish eyes animals have when they're sad or in pain. No screams. Horses don't scream either. I gave her a drop of water with sugar in it, and she looked at me so gratefully. I helped her. The only thing I couldn't take was when she ate all the mess. I tried to clean her with a bit of rag.' They found the little girl asleep beside the puppies.

'I'm very primitive, I'm not at all far from my roots.' Her skin reflected the sun like some North African fruit. 'Coco, put your hat on,' her aunts shouted at her. 'You're so ugly with those Mameluke's cheekbones, but your complexion's not bad and you ought to look after it . . . Just like a Tartar,' they said to each other. The little girl waited till they'd gone and looked the word up in the dictionary. All she found was 'Russian steppe.' For the present, the only place she knew were the woods to which she escaped in the morning when the beds were spread to air overlooking the garden. The aunts' finicking eyes strayed no farther than their black imitation leather account-books. Coco took deep breaths of the seasons, from the hoar-frost to the faint scent of flowering buckwheat. Walking along the lanes, she imagined the gipsies would carry her off. 'For six years I waited for that to happen.' Or she would gallop at breakneck speed, till the mare's fanatic nostrils were covered in foam. Sometimes she would be accompanied by the redhead son of a farmer. He was scared. No, she told him, eyes gleaming, no one will know. It never entered her aunts' heads that she'd dare to ride the untamed creatures they never even saw. 'We had horses as others have cows.' The horses were reared for the cavalry, and the yearly visit by the quartermaster-general to buy remounts was a long-awaited and carefully prepared event. It was forbidden to ride horses that hadn't been shod: it caused a cleft to form between the hooves. The two culprits were in fear and trembling lest the inspectors should notice . . .

When the aunts thought Coco had run about long enough, they told her to learn to sew by making her trousseau. The servants did crochet-work, the aunts knitted babies' layettes. Coco tried hemming and seaming, but got worse rather than better. 'My aunts used to laugh at me for being so clumsy.'

In the evening they chased her out to be washed with kitchen soap. A cake of rose-scented soap, a present from one of her boy cousins, gave her a moment of intoxication. 'My cousin kissed me passionately. I let him, The frenzy of the provinces . . . I didn't see him again for three months. That's the sort of thing that makes a woman of one.' In the provinces it was one bath a week, on washing day. Coco wore a shift to be bathed – it was a sin to look at your body. She held her petticoat between her teeth as she put on her nightdress, and her nightdress between her teeth as she put on her petticoat. Well scrubbed all over, she would sit down to dinner, her mouth shut tight, her napkin folded in the shape of a mitre. Chinese bezique, a serial novel, and a basket of floss silk awaited her aunts, who sat with their feet on footwarmers filled with live charcoal mingled with ashes to keep it going. The maids used to sit round the table too, with their work. Coco could neither knit nor sew, but sat, head bent, working cross-stitch on her nightdresses to make them look Russian. Sometimes her aunts would suggest she should read Victor Hugo. 'That's why I can't bear him!' But she would do as she was told, nonetheless, and read Hugo aloud with much emphasis, pleased to be able to do something the maids couldn't. But soon, alas, her aunts would clap their hands: up to bed now.

Coco always retained her horror of the family curfew. It was the moment when the cats brushed past you: she hated cats. People in big houses had to have them to hunt the rats and break up their confabulations. 'They said a cat might jump on your chest while you're asleep and stifle you. I've never got over that.' She put a stick under the sheet, threw off the blanket, and made herself a tent. Beneath it she counted up her treasures, her five-franc pieces; if someone came in, she couldn't be taken by surprise. Already she had her private area, her unassailable refuge. The cook used to save candle-ends for her, but eventually the light burned down and the ghost lay in wait. Fear of the dark got the better of her. She was delicate, and had noticed that no one said anything if she called out in the night because of a nose-bleed. The local doctor suggested dousing her in the 'bachol,' the big vat full of water evaporating in the sun, used for grapes at wine-harvest. A cold bath on top of her tuberculosis – that was all she needed. Nervous and mischievous, she used to rub her nose just where it made it bleed. It was her bloodstained mother she was always marked with. No ritual washing during those disturbed nights at the Ritz could ever cleanse the spot.

'Too strict an education freezes the soul,' wrote Pierre Reverdy in *My Log-book*. It wouldn't have taken much to make the rebellious little girl melt. 'If anyone kissed me I wanted to cry. I held myself stiff so as to say good-bye properly. Pride saved me.' Her only wish was to cling in someone's arms, but she wasn't going to throw herself in those of the maids.

Her aunts used to take her to mass wearing toques on their heads with dangling jade ornaments, tight half-veils, and white edging round their throats; they carried heavy prayer-books in their hands. She told them: 'You ought to wear big hats.' 'The child's mad,' they said. She hated their wooden pew and went to sit with the children from school. When she sang the *Ave Maria* and the *Tantum ergo* with too much enthusiasm, a nun would give her a poke with a stick. But her heart was in solitary confinement. She was in love with the hunchback. 'He used to sit on a bench. I'd have liked to sit down beside him and touch his hump and tell him it didn't matter, he could still be loved.'

Her senses, on the watch, corroborated her. 'I have marvellous hearing,' she used to say. 'I could hear the grass grow.'

She liked to know all about everything, and used to listen at doors. 'Charming!' One day she overheard a word whose echo desolated her: someone called her 'the orphan.' When she was quite tiny she saw a school of orphan girls go by in their black overalls, heard someone call them 'poor orphans,' and hid to weep over them. She knew her father lived a long way away. Her wildness and contrariness grew like weeds in a neglected garden, outside the realm of order enclosed by her aunts' brisk boots. She threw away wooden dolls but loved those she made out of rags. She didn't dress them; they stayed in their underwear. 'It was them I loved – my little girls.' Cinderella, people called her.

She adored the dress her father sent her from America for her first communion. It was all ruffles and lace; the imitation leather purse that went with it contained a string of pearls, and was obviously chosen by a tart. Coco was so enchanted she couldn't eat any dinner: her dress from America! The rosaries, one large, one small; layer on layer of billowing organdie petticoats. And a long veil. And silk stockings. 'I'd never seen silk stockings before, you see.' The little peasant girls wore caps, but she was going to have a wreath of roses. 'I thought to myself, my father must have a lady with very good taste. She had no taste whatsoever.'

Her aunts said the dress was too showy. But everything fitted except the shoes. The aunts sent for a pair with bobbles on from the 'Bon Marché.' Coco thought they were too frivolous and wouldn't wear them. 'I thought they were cheap.'

She'd been thrilled by the monk who conducted the three-day 'retreat' that preceded the children's first communion. Mendicant friars used to call on the parish priest; he hated them. They were barefoot, in down-at-heel sandals and long homespun robes with a girdle – 'horrible, of course, but they talked differently.' The language they spoke was not like that of the parish priest – it was nearer the *caca en la vigna* of the Auvergnats. 'I got out the governess-cart and harnessed the horse.' There were no cars. (Coco told how the first car took the geese by surprise. Just a shower of feathers. No wonder a fool is called a goose.) 'When I got there – the monk and his bare feet and his oration. That was the life I'd been waiting for. Inside the church it was like a mirage. It got dark at five, the candles were lit, I could hear the breathing of the boys and girls around me, in the half-light, almost asleep. I said at confession afterwards it had inspired profane feelings in me.' The good curé gave a start: 'Where did you get hold of that expression? I thought you weren't so stupid as the others.' 'The Catholic religion crumbled for me. I realised I was a person, outside all the secrecy of confession.' Coco grew a head taller that day, and refused to do the stations of the cross as a penance in front of the other girls, all looking on intently between their fingers. 'I'll do it in bed,' she said. 'You're a rebel,' said the priest.

Her aunts had disapproved of all this showing-off. But they were flattered too. 'Right up to the last minute I was afraid they'd make me wear a little cap, but no, I wore my veils, and believe me . . . ! Ax had only three hundred inhabitants, and all the others were farmers, my aunts' tenants.' The cook told her she looked as pretty as a bride. 'I was intoxicated. And somehow I had to walk in all those things.' To keep up her courage she ate a cherry. Then: 'Aunt, aunt, quick, I must see the curé before the ceremony – I have to confess.' 'What have you done, you silly girl?' The aunts were most intrigued. Coco, on the verge of hysterics, knelt in the sacristy and confessed about the cherry. 'What, foolish child,' said the curé, 'do you mean to say you bothered me for that?' He made a sign of absolution over her head.

The little village girls, snub-nosed, shared out the little cakes cut into shapes: 'I want two men.' 'I only like dogs.' Kirsch took over from sweets. 'Wouldn't the young lady like a small glass?' 'Yes, please,' said the young lady.

Uncle Paul was a minor station-master, and occasionally sent a railway ticket. First class. 'Because I wouldn't go second class – it was a bore.' When Coco and her sister arrived at Uncle Paul's, their aunt, their father's sister, was cold and distant. The uncle was kind and came to kiss them good night in bed. 'You'll stay a nice long time, won't you?' 'No, we're going to-morrow. Auntie doesn't . . .' She still felt the chill of this premature attempt at self-control: 'Not to have any family left – to be pitied.' That feeling never diminished.

She went to spend a month's holiday with her sister at the convent of Notre-Dame de la Vallette in Corrèze. The food was awful, not like at the aunts'. 'My aunts didn't eat much, but they paid reverence to meals, saluted each dish as it was served. In the provinces the cook is respected. There's always a proper meal. In case anyone comes . . .' The nuns indulged in shuttlecock and other foolish pastimes. Coco accompanied their heavenly notes on the organ, and sang. The nuns, country girls, were amazed. 'When my sister had been playing the piano they used to look at her fingers to see what she had on the ends of them. Little peasants!' Many years later Coco sent Jansen there to see the beautiful black and white tiled staircase, to copy for her house at Roquebrune, where she also had convent doors put in. It was a Shakespearean house, full of blue irises and white arum lilies standing out against dazzling walls.

At sixteen and a half her sister left the convent and was married. But provincial life and its absolutism, wicked stepmother of freedom, couldn't wear out the rebelliousness of the intemperate little sister. She used to slide down four floors on the banisters, drunk with independence, thinking, 'I care for nobody, I do as I please.' One day she thought she'd hurt herself. But the maids told her aunts her nightdresses were stained. 'I was hauled before the court!' She'd reached puberty.

'They educated me but they taught me nothing. Only to become a hypocrite and hide all I felt. I remember when they used to take my knickers down to spank me. First there was the humiliation. Then it was very unpleasant, your bottom was red as blood. And now go up to bed, they said.' But a knout would not break the spirit of that little Tartar. 'I read everything I could lay hands on.' When some young officers, 'chasseurs alpins' in uniforms of sky-blue and astrakhan, appeared, and one came to dinner, she loosened her plaits so that her hair fluffed out nicely, and came down with shining eyes. But her aunts wouldn't let her dine with the grown-ups. She sobbed her heart out when she was thirteen and her aunts took her to Paris to see Sarah Bernhardt in *La Dame aux camélias*. Like true provincials they went in the summer because it was cheaper and there were extra items on the programme. 'We got in at the Gare de Lyon and stayed at the Terminus Hotel at the Gare Saint-Lazare. The heat! I hated it. I could hardly walk on the thick nailed-down carpets – I was used to polished floors.'

She sobbed into her handkerchief. '*La Dame aux camélias* was my life, all the trashy novels I'd fed on.' The rest of the audience, also up from the country, complained and wanted to turn her out. Her aunts threatened her, but she came back to see Bernhardt play 'L'Aiglon' with her wooden leg. Coco still loved her old-fashioned portrait, fawn-coloured in the Petit Palais.

'I was in black. It looked nice, with my white collar. In the provinces you wear your mourning until it falls off you in pieces! People told my aunts I ought to have another dress. "But she's an orphan," they said. "When she's sixteen we'll see." '

Her lungs were delicate and her aunts sent her to board with the keeper of the Arcachon basin near Bordeaux. 'I've got T.B.,' she told the peasants in Auvergne, 'and I'm going to see the sea.' In the morning she hurtled down the stairs to go to the oyster-beds with the 'boss'; he opened an oyster for her with his knife, but she wouldn't eat it. But he went on preparing them for the young lady, and swallowing them himself. Her cheeks and hands burned almost black by sun and wind, she smiled at him with all her span of white teeth, like a little squaw. 'You look like a cannibal,' they told her when she went home. She never forgot the sea-meadow full of scabious, and the rough sea glimpsed through purple thistles on the dunes. 'I'm going to look at the storm,' she told the keeper's wife, who reminded her not to forget her shoes – she only had one pair left. She was to lose them again with Dali.

Gala, a worrier, needed another stamp on her visa and left Arcachon for Bordeaux. Coming back from the station, Coco and Dali went down to the dunes, which he'd never seen. 'He only knew the house and the station.' They left their shoes on the sand and couldn't find them. Dali capered about, and Coco saw all their friends from the Russian ballet among the trees. 'Diaghilev, Lifar, they were all there following us.'

Coco and Dali

She always remained the same solitary romantic. She hated squalor and Victor Hugo, and was dazzled by the novels of Pierre Decourcelle – the rebel with the softness of the dunes. 'Everything that was the opposite of what I knew seemed enviable.' With beating heart, she thought only of how to escape from her aunts. 'People imagine all doors opened before me, but I pushed them open. I'm as idle as a snake, but I've never let myself be chained. Any loop-hole will do. As long as you've got something to eat and drink, and know you've got somewhere to sleep . . .'

But from her sturdy native province, from her stock, she retained a respect for work, the integrity of a task well done. 'My aunts taught me cleanliness, regularity, decency, and above all not to speak with an accent. I'll always be grateful to them for that. Imagine having the same accent as Pierre Laval!' Sometimes the little girl used to speak the local patois, and Coco would still do the same: 'God dang me if I let those devils get the better of me!' Her aunts used to tell her: 'We do all we can, Coco, but if you start speaking patois . . .' Somewhere deep inside her her grandfather grumbled away still: 'Not worth the shoes on a dog.' She told me: 'I was very disappointed there wasn't a special dress for people who made clothes. I thought it would be the same for couturiers as for shoe-makers. It helped people to know where they were.' She always respected the honour of the guild, of her staff. Once the doors were pushed open and she had taken flight, the rebel, her little hat on her head, was ready to bow to others.

To '*faire Chanel*' was the family expression for withdrawing to some self-supporting property. Coco did it several times over. 'You have to be known in order to be acknowledged.' Recognition was what she had been searching for ever since the empty region of her childhood. It would be her refuge, in which she could take countless revenges. In her aunts' house there were no mirrors. You had to scramble over the furniture to squint at yourself in a scrap of glass. Coco had mirrors everywhere. She used them as wallpaper. And the

'Coco had mirrors everywhere' – here in the Faubourg Saint-Honoré

fragrance unknown to her childhood revealed her wherever she went. 'If anyone speaks to you of your perfume it must be someone who's come quite close to you.' Her hatred of hair? 'Hair means the family to me. Where does yours come down to? All I ever saw was long hair hanging down nightdresses. It's so out-of-date.' Above all, hair was the smell her father disliked, in the rare kisses of remembrance.

Her father's English, his girl-friend's taste, the breath-taking dress which was the greatest happiness of her child-hood, all foreshadowed her escape to England and the ever-repeated task. Her first communion dress was the only pleasure she could remember of her father. She never heard of him again. In all the thousands of dresses that were to come, she would clothe women in her own emotion, en-deavouring to make them less likely to be deserted, never resigning herself to that primal desertion. Throughout the litany of her collections she kept alive her communion dress, the only one that dressed Coco herself with love.

Julia, her sister, was unhappy. 'She only loved the convent,' said Coco. Worst of all, she found out that her husband had not given up his mistress, and killed herself by opening her veins, leaving the little son whom Coco and Boy Capel sent for. Coco wanted a child by Boy, but her small womb was impenetrable. A midwife attempted an operation, which failed. Jean-Louis Faure, the surgeon, was sent for urgently. Boy found her looking sunburnt. 'Have you been in the country?' he asked. No, she had taken the air in the little garden of the clinic in the rue de la Chaise. She could never have a child.

A friend, she told me with her habitual reserve, wanted to take her to the cinema, but she said she'd rather wait till things stopped dancing about. 'Do me the favour of letting me take you to my oculist,' he said. 'When?' she asked eagerly. 'To-morrow.' She had faulty convergence and only one-third vision, with which she saw what she wanted to see and ignored the rest: 'One eye swears at the other.' The oculist

'If I had to choose one unforgettable and unique feature in a person,
it would be the eyes . . . her eyes remained intent and vulnerable.'

was indignant that her family hadn't bothered about it.
'Family! What there was of it! My aunts told me off for pulling
faces.' When she went out to dinner at Maxim's wearing long-
distance glasses for the first time, 'I almost cried out, people
looked so ugly. I was seeing them as they are for the first
time, instead of in my imagination.'

If I had to choose one unforgettable and unique feature in a
person, in Coco it would be the eyes. Many others would
select her tongue and her unparalleled boldness. But her eyes
remained intent and vulnerable.

The death of Boy, her only love, linked up with the primal destiny, the cell formed by the death of her mother. Henceforth Coco could never free herself of regret. Her terrific courage could do nothing against her fundamental fear. Her generative strength, the strength of a lion, could not drive out the scene of childhood. 'There's something in the human presence,' she said to me, 'that you don't understand. If I could see everything around me which is hostile, it would be terrible.' She barricaded the doors of her hotel room against all intrusion, against any invasion of the secret and derisory treasure of her solitude. Any attempt was an ambush.

Deep down, she needed to defend herself. She cut, adjusted and measured. Her mind used scissors too, and was implacable. Her need to hurt in order to make sure she was loved, her constant denunciation – both were forms of retaliation. Her aggressivity showed above the surface, but quickly turned into the loneliness of the long-distance runner. Her plundering ego was linked to the broken thread of the past.

Graham Greene has written that inside us we are always the same age. One day when I arrived at the studio, where she was distributing materials among her cutters and the unchanging Madame Raymonde, astute and round as her necklace in her white overall – 'Yes, Mam'zelle,' 'Of course, Mam'zelle' – she deliberately unleashed a storm. 'You're not a countrywoman,' she said to me. 'It's just that the sheep have got the staggers.' Of the white stockings crossed in the rue Cambon: 'I prefer the real white stockings the maids used to wear at home.' The curtains were of turkey-red cotton, the same that swelled with the night-time fears of childhood. Coco could still remember the braid women wore round the hem of their skirts to protect them from the wax on the floors. The old Auvergne friend who gave her the topaz, her lucky charm, used to keep her skirts clear of the floor with a chain. This fascinated Coco. 'Perhaps that's where my fondness for chains comes from.' Bunches of keys, medals, seals – she used to hook them all on the chain round her waist.

The once-forbidden mirrors lined her walls and reflected her metamorphosis. Her marvellous things, her travelling companions, her magic animals, were always with her. They were her atoms, she charged herself and protected herself with them, they were the intercessors between her and the supremacy of life. But what was lost always lurked there; she was always listening after it. It was everywhere, after that first, initial want. The inner threshold was never crossed. Among those solid, opaque objects, Coco was surrounded by exiles. Her attempt to please, the rare rites she devoted to the body, only reflected back illusion and were stopped short by the screen memory: deeper down was the secret destiny, unconscious of its loss, which served as basic motivation for the other. True, success in the task undertaken constituted a reassurance, after the bleeding of the mother and the father's desertion, a loss of which Coco bore the mark in her delicate lungs. But the resonance of childhood remained open-mouthed, unassuaged. Her metaphor led her back at the end of the road to solitude, to the early lack she always tried to escape. There would be no reunion. At the moment when images are fixed for ever on the implacable film, a little girl was unloved.

Now she didn't give herself nose-bleeds any more. She had run away, with her solitude. But the bread of her childhood still stuck in her throat. And her violence was love, the love of a girl waiting with her ear pressed against the door.

'I've always thought I'd start to live when I stopped being like a child.' But it was late. Almost night.

1st January, 1971. Coco was alone at the Ritz. 'Waiting is my occupation,' she said. She kept away from all the fuss she hated, the Christmas tree with all the tables round it.

'This evening they're going to eat the tree. New Year – the

187

very words disgust me. And it upsets business completely. The only thing is not to give a damn about anything – otherwise, just disillusion and frustration.' She burned with resentment at not being able to work that day. She wanted to abandon fashion. 'I've finished with them once and for all. My system is to do nothing. To-morrow you'll find me in the rue Cambon.'

To-morrow was Sunday.

Coco didn't want to have anything more to do with anything, and had gone to earth in her room at the Ritz, waiting for it to be time for work. Should I have recognised, in her iniquitous sense of aggression, in this withdrawal and retreat like an animal reduced to its own territory, the obscure intuition that tormented her? Her days were numbered. But I thought it was only the familiar lengthening of her defences, made more intense by the approach of her collection and the reserves she needed to accumulate, now as ever, so as to be able to see it through. In short, I was blind to what obstinately characterised her: her horror of dates, of domination, of the rendezvous not given by love. It was the rendezvous with death.

She was deep in Erlanger's *Richelieu*. 'The best story there is is the history of France. I prefer real history to a bad novel.' The trashy novel she used to love in her youth was a thing of the past. But she still felt a certain nostalgia. 'It's better than Alexandre Dumas,' she said of her book, 'but it hasn't got so much passion . . .' Her favourite was Louis XIII, king at thirteen years old. His mother didn't love him. 'The people he made rich, the Luynes, hated and fleeced him,' she said in disgust. Then, more mildly: 'When he loved a woman he sent her to a convent. He went to war on his horse . . .'

Chanel went to the rue Cambon. On the eve of her death she was at work. 'What are you going to put on the shoulders? Nothing. Your suit's a wash-out.' Manon brought a suit: 'I took her on as an errand-girl when she was twenty. All this pink . . . who said you could choose the lining? You can't start lining a suit until it sits properly!' Out of the blouses proposed to her, she chose the cambric one because cambric isn't draughty and washes well. 'You can't wear a blouse twice – impossible.' She called for jersey: 'I invented it, and I'm not having it filched from me . . . It doesn't spoil. I'm against scenes with maids. They're the princesses of our age. You need a dress you can put on a hanger when you get home. It mustn't spoil – a dirty uniform is terrible. A dress is not just a rag, it's an object.'

An object. A love object. Love reappeared under the wool, which she found unsatisfactory. 'You must be able to see her body underneath, otherwise she gets lost in her suit. Where's the woman? With me, fashion will never be a matter of long or short skirts. To impose a length . . . I won't do to others what I wouldn't have them do to me!' She adjusted the hat: 'You mustn't jam it on, it's just to shelter your eyes. And I don't want to see too much hair. Draw it back so it can't be seen and the face is small. As soon as the hair's drawn back, a face becomes noble.'

An evening dress was boring. 'We're not working for a convent. Give me some black lace.' She swathed the legs in lace trousers under the transparent muslin. 'I won't be any more immodest than that . . .'

Madame Raymonde lifted the tape with the scissors from round her neck. 'I don't like the country,' she said to her fore-women. 'What I like is driving off along the roads.'

She was to die the next day, a Sunday, the day she hated. I arrived at the Ritz at one o'clock and found her at her dressing-table, in her white silk pyjama trousers, her currant-coloured blouse, a little snood and a bow on her hair, making herself up. 'You see,' she said to me, 'I would have gone to the rue Cambon to-day, even for only two people. I shan't be able to resist,' she said wistfully, 'making that dress with a bustle like the one my mother wore . . . Jeanne!' she called to Céline, clearing up after her mistress's morning bath. She changed from pyjamas into stockings; they should always, she told me, be the same colour as the skin. She inspected her legs and went back to the dressing-table to put some cream and powder on them, showing me how they caught the sun where they emerged from the white towelling mules. Coco fled even the transparent sunlight that came through the window of her luxury attic. 'If one had to do all this pruning for someone else – not a chance. But one does it for oneself.' She posed in front of the mirrors, and I thought I discerned an appeal made by her body, something profound, untamed, a challenge that still had something to do with desire. That evening it would breathe its last.

She put on her long white silk panties – 'for if your skirt rides up a bit' – and rejected the suit Céline offered. 'No, the other one.' 'I was keeping that for the collection, Mademoiselle.' Coco took the remaining one – there were only three in the wardrobe. 'The beige blouse would have been better, but still . . .'

She sat in front of the dressing-table mirror and put on her hat – 'Not so as to smother everything' – and noticed she'd forgotten to do her eyebrows. So she took the hat off, and did them in her make-up mirror. Vivacious and lovely, she stood up, her hat on her curls again, slipped her necklets under her belt, one in her pocket, and as always put some pancake make-up on her hands and powdered them.

'Call the carriage,' she told Céline, meaning the lift, and swallowed a glass of sugar and water and a Nopirin. 'To-morrow I'll use my gold plate. It's not pretentious – my place is not pretentious at all. The only thing is, the knives make scratches on it. I'll just use the gold for cheese plates – there's no need to saw away at cheese. I like the colour of gold.'

We had lunch at her usual table, out of the way, independent, free from the smells. Monsieur Ritz bowed. Coco ordered her famous unsalted ham to start with, followed by a minute steak with boiled potatoes, a melon for dessert, and the customary well-chilled Riesling. 'I caught romanticism from novels. As for finding it in real life . . .' A coffee. The other people in the restaurant disappeared. 'They're off to Long-champ,' she explained. We lingered, the last to go. 'You must experience passion. I'll sense it right away. You'll be a bit worn out, and satisfied. Even if it only lasts a fortnight. Because then I'll stop you. I always went off . . .'

She put on her coat of tweed lined with kalgan. 'It's ten years old,' she said. Washable beige gloves, open at the wrist. The Cadillac drove up the Champs-Elysées, crammed with a gloomy crowd, and took us on 'her' drive: round the race-course in a mist pierced by a blinding sun. 'I hate the setting sun, this light. I should have brought my dark glasses.' We came back past Trocadéro. Coco remembered the Musée de l'Homme and the fragility of human features, and clicked her teeth. 'Castanets . . . My teeth are chattering with fear.' In the Place de la Concorde, among the stone statues of the provinces, I saw her bow. 'I'm saluting the moon.' It was full. 'Oh, dear, I forgot to do my tiercé,' she mused.

I left her at the door of the Ritz. 'I'll be working to-morrow.'

The final warning came on her when she was lying down, ordering her evening meal. Feeling unwell suddenly, she tried to give herself her injection, but her hands shook too much to break the phial. Céline broke it for her. She told me after-wards she'd never seen Mademoiselle give herself her injec-tion so violently. She was in pain. 'You see,' she said to Céline. 'This is how one dies.' Her ruling lucidity had helped her. Alone.

She looked very small under the white Ritz sheet drawn up to her heart. You couldn't see her hands. On her bedside table were Stravinsky's icon, *Richelieu*, and Malraux's *Antimémoires*. Céline had dressed her in the white blouse and the suit which she wore every day. The dazzling scarf had become a linen handkerchief tied under the chin to keep it in place. Her skeleton, that of a little girl taking her first communion, was at rest. The imp of violence inhabited her no more.

> *Dis qu'as-tu fait, toi que voilà,*
> *Dis, qu'as-tu fait de ta jeunesse?*

The lines of Verlaine that she loved kept vigil over her.

> Tell me, you there, what have you done,
> What have you done with your youth?

At the church of the Madeleine, all the wreaths were white. Only Luchino Visconti's was of red roses and camellias. Orchids abounded as sheaves of flowers were left – a cushion of camellias, a shield woven of laurel leaves with her scissors on it in lilac, and a rosette of ribbon with the words: 'Your models.' Standing beside it, a cross of white azaleas recalled those cut in the Westminster hothouses: on the bow of ribbon was written 'François.' The priest recited the prayer of the Father and Son. Only her family gave the blessing. Perhaps she would have liked that, she who all her life had no family.

She was no longer Coco, no longer Chanel. She was 'Gabrielle thy servant,' in accordance with the Catholic liturgy, in the last rendezvous of one who never agreed to be there. The priest omitted the secular name her parents had added to her baptismal name. They had called her Gabrielle Bonheur. Gabrielle Happiness.